"Frequently surprising and always enlightening, *Lastingness* has a style that mixes the eloquent and the rueful in about equal measure, and in all its paragraphs the book is both learned and wise."
    —Charles Baxter, author of *The Feast of Love*

"From where else but the panoramic cultural erudition of Nicholas Delbanco could such a tour de force of artistic sensitivity have come? This book is an engaging course in twentieth century Western humanities and a literary gift to its readers."
    —Shewin Nuland, author of *How We Die*

For *The Lost Suitcase*

"Like the veteran and enormously accomplished storyteller that he is, Nicholas Delbanco, in this gathering of eight elegant essays and the brilliant virtuosity of the title novella, tells us tales that soon become parables and move us to laughter and sadness, to admiration and praise. *The Lost Suitcase* is a wonderful book, ablaze with talent and stunning in its impeccable integrity."
    —George Garrett, author of *Death of the Fox*

"Nicholas Delbanco's book of narrative riffs and meditations is a wonder. He may know more than just about anyone about the serious play that is literary life, and he writes of it with great spirit and flair."
    —Lorrie Moore, author of *Birds of America*

"Delbanco writes brilliantly about how literary art is achieved. He teaches as he writes, and he does so grippingly; the drama, which serious writing actually is, becomes manifest on his pages."
    —Frederick Busch, author of *The Night Inspector*

ALSO BY NICHOLAS DELBANCO

FICTION

The Years

Sherbrookes: One Volume

The Count of Concord

Spring and Fall

The Vagabonds

What Remains

Old Scores

In the Name of Mercy

The Writers' Trade & Other Stories

About My Table & Other Stories

Stillness

Sherbrookes

Possession

Small Rain

Fathering

In the Middle Distance

News

Consider Sappho Burning

Grasse 3/23/66

The Martlet's Tale

21ST CENTURY ESSAYS

David Lazar and Patrick Madden, Series Editors

Curiouser and Curiouser

ESSAYS

Nicholas Delbanco

Mad Creek Books, an imprint of
The Ohio State University Press
Columbus

Published by Mad Creek Books, an imprint of The Ohio State University Press.

Library of Congress Cataloging-in-Publication Data

Names: Delbanco, Nicholas, author.
Title: Curiouser and curiouser / Nicholas Delbanco.
Other titles: 21st century essays.
Description: Columbus : Mad Creek Books, an imprint of The Ohio State
    University Press, [2017] | Series: 21st century essays
Identifiers: LCCN 2017008605 | ISBN 9780814254165 (pbk. ; alk. paper) | ISBN
    0814254160 (pbk. ; alk. paper)
Classification: LCC PS3554.E442 A6 2017 | DDC 814/.54—dc23
LC record available at https://lccn.loc.gov/2017008605

Cover design by Nathan Putens
Text design by Juliet Williams
Type set in Adobe Garamond Pro

9 8 7 6 5 4 3 2 1

For Anna, Penelope, Rosalie, Frederica, and Lydia
Grand granddaughters, all

"Curiouser and Curiouser!" cried Alice.

—Lewis Carroll, *Alice's Adventures in Wonderland*

CONTENTS

Author's Note: The first of these five essays is the first I wrote in the new millennium; the final section of the final piece is the most recent. This arrangement is not chronological, however, but an attempt to represent a different kind of continuum: from music to the visual arts to the literary life. The taut-stretched line between the private and public arena is one I here attempt to walk, and it is this author's hope that his personal take on the balance between them is not a circus act.

CURIOUSER AND CURIOUSER

The Countess of Stanlein Restored

On 22 September 1998, the cellist Bernard Greenhouse drove from his home in Massachusetts the five hours south to Manhattan. On the car's rear seat reposed his prized possession, named in honor of two of its previous owners: the "Countess of Stanlein ex-Paganini" Stradivarius violoncello of 1707. Strapped down and secure in its carrying case, the instrument traveled wherever he went, and it had done so for years. This afternoon, however, he was planning to realize a long-deferred dream and deposit the "Strad" in New York.

It did require work. There were nicks and scratches scattered on the surface, front and back. The varnish had thickened and darkened in spots; in others the varnish had thinned. Some previous patches needed retouching; in places the edging had cracked. The glue by the sound post—an old repair—leaked. Decades of pressure on the neck and from the downward force of the bridge-feet beneath the taut-stretched strings had warped the f-holes into less than perfect symmetry; the ribs would need to be adjusted and the front plate aligned.

Not all of this was visible, and only the discerning eye would notice or, noticing, object. The instrument had long been famous for both its beauty and tone. But Greenhouse is a perfectionist, and previous repairs had been stopgap and partial, in the service of utility. At the height of his career he performed—with the Bach Aria Group, as a founding member of the Beaux Arts Trio, as soloist and on recordings—more than two hundred times per year. From continent to continent, in all sorts of weather and playing conditions the Countess of Stanlein had been his companion; he carried her on boats and planes, in rented cars and taxicabs and trains, and always in a rush.

Now the career was winding down. No longer appearing routinely in concert, he owned several other instruments to practice on at home. At eighty-two, the cellist had the money and unscheduled time and the desire to "give back," as he put it, "something of value" to the world of music that had given him so much. This was to be, he reasoned, both a good deed and an investment. He knew just the man to do the job—René Morel, on West 54th Street—and the work had been agreed upon and delivery date arranged.

Greenhouse had been a student of the late Pablo Casals. After the Second World War he traveled to Prades, in the French Pyrenees, where the Catalan cellist lived in retirement. As a protest against Generalissimo Franco, Casals accepted no public engagements but continued, in private, to work at his art; there, in the church of San Miguel de Cuxa, he recorded the six Unaccompanied Suites for Violoncello by Johann Sebastian Bach. There too, in 1946, he took on the young American as an apprentice. More than a half century later, that audition stays vivid for Greenhouse.

"He started asking for the repertoire, and he requested many pieces. After an hour or more of my playing—during which he indicated nothing more than the piece and the passage he wanted me to play—he said, 'All right. Put down your cello, put it away, and we'll talk.' He said to me, 'Well, what you need is an apprenticeship to a great artist. I believe in the apprentice system. Stradivari, Guarneri, Amati: they turned out so many wonderful violin makers. And I believe the same thing can hold true in making musicians. If I knew of a great artist I could send you to, I would do so,' he said, 'because my mind is very much occupied with the Spanish Republican cause. But since I don't know whom to send you to—and if you agree to stay in the village and take a lesson at least once every two days—I will teach you.'"

Such a system of tutelage remains in place today: implicit in the idea of "master classes" and explicit in the trade of the luthier. This is a generic term for those who make and repair bowed stringed instruments, and the enterprise feels nearly medieval in its hierarchy of apprentice, journeyman laborer, master craftsman. Young men still clean the varnish rags or sweep wood shavings from the floor as did their predecessors centuries ago, and under much the same close watchful supervision. Bernard Greenhouse met René Morel in the early 1950s when the luthier was working for the legendary Fernando Sacconi in the New York shop of Rembert Wurlitzer; he commended the Frenchman thereafter to the dealer Jacques Français. In 1994 Morel struck out on his own, as both dealer and restorer. His long and narrow workroom is chock-a-block with wood and tools and objects in molds and on benches; his public rooms display memorabilia— signed concert posters and photographs of virtuosi—from the storied past.

What this luthier sells are violins and violas and cellos and bows of value and importance, and what he repairs is the *crème de la crème*. There are workaday instruments also, of course; nearly a thousand pass through the shop each year for sale or repair. A dealer's reputation, however, rests on the highest common denominator of stock—and to have handled the Countess of Stanlein is no small professional thing. Greenhouse and Morel admire each other cordially; they trust each other a little, and when the cellist delivered his instrument for the purpose of "restoration," he left with a two-by-three-inch numbered ticket as receipt.

*

The human animal makes lists. Instinctively we scan the charts for those who come first, second, last. We like to know the names of the ten best- or worst-dressed celebrities, the all-time all-star baseball team, the richest men or women, the twelve safest cities for family life, and the millennium's five or five hundred most important citizens. We rank colleges and wines. In our obsessive calibration of achievement by degrees, there are tables and annotated lists of lists; it sometimes seems as though the need to establish a "top dog" or "leader of the pack" stays programmed in the species. Hierarchy has its comforts, after all; we want to know where we belong and, by extrapolation, where we stand.

Such ranking in terms of artistic achievement is a thankless task. We may have heavyweight champions of the world and world leaders in automobile or oil production, but enter the domain of art and any assessment of primacy falls flat. Pick the "greatest" of composers and for every proponent of Bach there will be a Beethoven buff; urge Mozart as the supreme musical consciousness and you'll find an adept of Stravinsky and one of Schubert or Schumann and one of Paul Simon or Sting. Pick the "greatest" of visual artists and there'll be votes cast in that beauty contest for Raphael and Rembrandt and da Vinci and Dürer and Grandma Moses and Andy Warhol and Monet. Even Shakespeare has detractors: those who would put him in context or believe that he couldn't be Shakespeare or prefer Milton instead. The marketplace requires multiplicity, and to insist that X outranks Y is to reveal mere personal preference or a set of cultural blinders; a declension of the hundred "best books" or "all-time favorite" love songs seems on the face of it inane.

For there can be no argument—no instructive disagreement—as to taste. *De gustibus non est disputandum* is a dictum accepted by all. Yet ask a hundred people to name the greatest of instrument makers, and ninety-five will agree. One name is preeminent, and those who challenge his reputation do so as iconoclasts. If you have heard of anyone, you will have heard of Stradivari, and to propose Guadagnini or Gofriller or members of the Amati family as the most accomplished of luthiers is to cast a protest vote. (Guarneri del Gesù has his consequential advocates, and there are cognoscenti who prize his violins and violas above all others, but he died young and worked at speed and built, it would seem, only one cello. To project what would have happened had he continued making violoncellos is beside the present point.) I know of no artist or craftsman more universally honored than is Stradivari; his bowed wooden stringed instruments have long been celebrated as the Platonic ideal of the form.

*

Antonio Stradivari was born in or near Cremona, Italy, in 1644. The actual date and place of his birth have been lost, but various Stradivaris had prospered in Cremona for centuries before. (The Latin and Italian spelling of his patronymic—*Stradivarius* and *Stradivari*—are interchangeable; by convention the former refers to an instrument, the latter to its maker, but this is a distinction long-since blurred. Indeed, the proper orthography was *Stradiuarius* until in 1730 the luthier himself replaced the *u* with a roman *v*. One of his violin-making sons retained it; another returned to the *u*.) Ottolinus Stradivari had been a *senator patriae* as early as 1127; in 1186 there was a senator named Egidius Stradivari; the lawyer Guglielmus Stradivertis died in 1439. In the 1630s and 1640s, however, bubonic plague swept through Cremona, and those who could afford to do so moved to nearby countryside; during plague years recordkeeping was in any case at risk.

We know a good deal about the instrument maker nevertheless, and this itself attests to his prominence. *Ricco come Stradivari* was a saying of the Cremonese vernacular, and it referred not to inheritance but earnings. He did well. The master craftsman lived long and was proud of longevity; in 1736 he inscribed a violin now called the "Muntz" Stradivarius with a label in his own hand, claiming to be ninety-two years old. (His first such label, in which he describes himself as a pupil of Amati, was signed in 1666.) So our knowledge of the birth date is in effect retrospective, a matter of subtraction, and whether he was born in Cremona or Brescia or Bergamo remains, as of this writing, moot.

He worked till the day of his death, and that day *was* recorded.

In the year of our Lord one thousand seven hundred and
thirty-seven on the nineteenth day of the month of December,
Signor Antonio Stradivari, a widower, aged about ninety-five
years, having died yesterday, fortified by the holy sacraments
and comforted by prayers for his soul until the moment he
expired, I, Domenico Antonio Strancari, parish priest of this
church of Saint Matteo, have escorted today his corpse with
funeral pomp to the church of the very reverend fathers of
Saint Domenico in Cremona, where he was buried.[1]

We think that we know what he looked like—tall, dark, fine-
fingered—though there's no authenticated likeness; we're told he
wore a white cap routinely, and a white leather apron at work.
We believe that he was pious, self-effacing, not litigious. These
last qualities, however, are more a function of evidence absent
than present; for so long-lived and prosperous a citizen to have
engaged in so few court proceedings must mean he stayed con-
tentedly at home and in his shop. Lately his testament has been
unearthed; we know the size of his estate—in a word, considerable—and what he distributed where. The dates of his two mar-
riages also have been recorded—to Francesca Ferabosca, a widow,
and, when he in turn became a widower, to Antonia Zambelli—
then the names of his several children, their birth dates, and
which of them grew up.

We deduce from the signed label ("*Antonius Stradiuarius Cre-
monensis, Alumnus Nicolais Amati, Faciebat Anno 1666*") that
he was apprenticed to Nicolo Amati and an "alumnus" of his
shop; we assume that he lived, as well as plied his trade, at Piazza
Roma, #1. He probably hung his instruments to dry in the attic
of this building, but the structure no longer exists. As is the case
with Shakespeare, the provincial place that harbored him at first
appeared indifferent; his bones were removed from the crypt of
the church when the church itself was razed; his workshop too

was leveled and his tools and patterns dispersed. Now Cremona celebrates its honored resident and ancient cottage industry with a museum of the violin, a festival devoted to violin making, and a tourism boom.

*

René Morel's hair is white and curly, his figure trim in a blue smock, and he rolls back his shirtsleeves meticulously and sports a close-barbered moustache. In his late sixties, Gallic and dapper, the luthier maintains his eleventh-floor workshop in New York's theater district. Outside the locked glass door of his studio, young dancers and singers and actors rehearse, and he eyes them where they cluster in the hall. "Those girls are wearing dental floss, not even a G-string," he says. "*Ces jeunes gens là,*" he says; "they entertain me with their dream of entertainment; they have not the slightest idea how hard one has to work."

He himself, he says, works very hard; his father and grandfather made instruments and he himself has been elected President of the *Entente Internationale des Maitres Luthiers et Archetiers d'Art*—Violin and Bow Makers. His assistants call him *Maître,* and he reports with pride that long ago Pablo Casals called him *Maître* Morel. He had been taken to the hotel where the famed artist was staying, then was introduced as the young man who could "save" the cello Casals would perform on that night. "And Sasha [Alexander Schneider] says, 'He's young but you'll see what he can do for you.' So Casals comes up and Martita, his wife, was with him. I turned red, yellow, and he called me *Maître* Morel. I was looking for a mousehole to hide in, I shook, I was very much in awe and I said, 'Oh, Maestro Casals if you call me *Maître* then how may I address you?' 'You must call me Pablo,' he says."

In Morel's own atelier—its proper name is Morel & Gradoux-Matt, Inc., since a Swiss luthier is his partner—dozens of instruments wait for repair. They range from the amateur's hand-me-down "cigar-box" to the professional's ideal of excellence. In the former case he lets his assistants do the work, murmuring *"Bien"* if he approves or pointing out in no uncertain terms what needs to be redone. In the latter instance—when the instrument is of particular interest or of particular value—he does the work himself. And restoration, it's worth repeating, differs from repair. Repair may be accomplished rapidly—a small adjustment of bridge or sound post in time for a concert, a brief application of glue and a clamp. But what he and Greenhouse contracted to do, within the limits of the possible, was full-fledged restoration, and this must be done with the instrument open, requiring patience and skill.

"When I was young," says Morel, "I could work twelve, fifteen hours at a time and never once be tired; my eyes were better then. But when you deal with restoration it cannot be hurried, it must not be rushed. To start with, we take it apart. Even so fine a lady as the Countess of Stanlein must be opened for examination. You insert the knife carefully, carefully just here into the glue—you must know how to do it—and then you just go *pop!*"

*

What are the components of this resonating box; what kind of wood is it made of and in what proportion? If this truly represents the Platonic ideal of the form of a violoncello, then how may we best measure it and who established its shape? Here's a skeletal description of the instrument's anatomy:

The *top* (alternately called the *table, belly,* or *front plate*) is typically made of two pieces of matching spruce or pine glued together. The inside of the top is graded from $3/16$ inches in the middle to $9/64$ inches at the edges, for a cello with a body length of 29½ inches. (Though Stradivari worked in centimeters, the standardized system of measure is English.) Two *f-holes*—so called because of their shape—are carved on the top of the instrument on each side; these are positioned by a proportion of 7:10 between the length of the neck and the distance from the upper edge of the top to the central notch of the f-holes.

The *back* is usually made of two matching pieces of maple—a harder wood than spruce or pine—selected for the figuration in and pattern of the wood. The back itself is graded from $4/16$ inches in the middle to $9/64$ inches at each edge. A few cellos exist with one-piece backs. The *neck, peg box,* and *scroll* were originally shaped from one piece of maple. The necks of older cellos were shorter than today's, but because of the rise in pitch over the centuries, new, longer necks have had to be grafted onto older instruments. When this is done, the peg box and scroll, an ornamental gesture on the part of the luthier, are retained if possible and replaced on the new neck.

There are *sides,* or *ribs*—six pieces of maple glued to the top and the back; there's a strip of light-colored wood glued between two strips of black wood to form one tripartite strip. This is called *purfling,* and six of these strips fit into a groove near the edge of each plate for purposes of decoration; they also protect the plate's edge. There's an elaborately carved piece of lightweight maple called a *bridge*; its feet are set—not glued—between the f-holes, centered on the f-hole notches, and it supports the four strings.

Over time such functional ornaments as an *end button,* a *nut,* and a *tailpiece* have become standard component parts of the instrument as well. The *end button* is a small, rounded piece of wood inserted into the end block with the cord of the tailpiece wrapped around it and a hole bored through the middle for a metal end pin. That end pin is adjustable, raising the instrument to its desired height and attaching to the floor. The carved triangular *tailpiece* is intended to keep the strings taut. The *nut,* slightly higher than the fingerboard, is a small piece of ebony glued onto the neck with grooves for proper spacing for the strings.

Interior component parts include the *linings,* the *bass bar,* and the *sound post.* The *linings* comprise twelve narrow strips of pine glued to the edges of the sides in order to increase the surface to which the top and back will be glued. The *bass bar* must be cut to fit the curvature of the top, then glued to the inside of the top on the left-hand side—where the lowest of the four strings, the

C-string, is positioned; therefore the bar is called *bass*. The *sound post* is not glued but placed just in front of the bridge's right foot, with ends shaped exactly to fit the contours of the top and back of the instrument; it sends the vibration from plate to plate, and its adjustment is crucial to the sound produced.

The end purpose of all such arrangements is, of course, sonority. The issues of weight and volume and proportion have to do with both the quality and quantity of noise produced. Too heavy an instrument fails to respond; too light a one will sound tinny or thin. The relatively slender walls of a guitar, for instance, will necessarily yield a different kind of vibration than those of a cello; sound waves result from density as well as from the volume of air contained by the wood's carved shape.[2]

*

I am the cellist's son-in-law; I have known him well by now for more than thirty years. In that time I have not known him to be separated from the instrument for more than a few weeks, when repair became imperative, and during that time—though playing a fine copy he had commissioned from the luthier Martin Cornellisen—he was restless. He admires the Cornellisen, as well as other instruments he owns (in particular a Contreras, known as the *Spanish Stradivarius*), but the Countess of Stanlein is his heart's darling, his beloved and best prized . . .

As with many other performers, stories attach to the matter of attachment: how Greenhouse lost the cello once, in transit, on a plane to Paris and found it in Vienna on the airport tarmac; how he left it in a taxi in Dubrovnik, and spent a sleepless night because the cabbie, once identified, said he himself required sleep and would return the cello in the morning; how he braved a machine-gun-wielding customs inspector in South America who wanted to subject the instrument to a strip search. (When Yo-Yo Ma misplaced his Montagnana in a New York taxi's trunk last year, it became a *cause célèbre* and its recovery a cause for celebration. Now his recorded voice inside the cab offers passengers the "classical advice" to remember their belongings.)

In early days of airplane travel, the Countess of Stanlein could come along free; then a "companion" ticket would be issued at half-price ("How old is your son Cello, Mr. Greenhouse?" an official in Newark once asked.) Then, with the increase in airplane traffic and procedural regulation, the cello's ticket became full-fare—it cannot, of course, be stowed in the hold—and now the instrument must travel in isolated splendor, strapped into its own wide padded seat in first class. The Russian soloist Raya Garbousova avoided that expensive inconvenience by calling her cello a *bass balalaika*; since airplane regulations made no mention of that instrument, she carried her Strad at no cost.

All such association entails accommodation, and habit entails a resistance to change. Since this musician and his cello have been inseparable for decades, performer and instrument fuse. Less a romantic vagary than statement of fact, such a process is familiar to any practiced player; the idiosyncrasies of an instrument, perplexing to **A,** have become second nature to **B.** And Morel knows how Greenhouse reacts.

"He was so fixed on the bridge Maestro Sacconi had cut for him that he wouldn't let it be moved. You ask him if I'm lying, it's probably been there now for thirty years and we spent fifteen years without moving the sound post either; of all my customers this is the one who has remained the longest with the same material. But Bernie, when he was younger and I first heard him play, he and his cello were one and one only; I always say there is no one in the world who could master that sound, it's *his* sound with the cello; you give that cello to anybody else and it won't sound the same. He has a way with the flesh of the finger, the vibrato of the hand—I was flabbergasted and I said to myself, that's it, that's the complete sound of this instrument."

The luthier's task, therefore, was twofold: to restore the physical object and not to alter the instrument's sound. This is a delicate balancing act, all the more so when musician and cello have been long-standing intimates. Unnumbered hours in rehearsal and performance make a millimeter's difference in the height of the bridge or the width of the neck loom large, and Greenhouse knows as if by instinct how to produce his particular tone. He and his instrument are—as Morel says admiringly—"one."

*

> The city of Cremona, capital of the Province of the same name, is of great antiquity, having been founded by the Romans in the year 218 BC . . . Whether or not Cremona is distinguished as the actual scene of the emergence of the true violin by the hands of Andrea Amati, founder of the Cremona School, or whether that honor should belong to the neighboring city of Brescia, where Gasparo da Salo also fashioned instruments of violin form in the sixteenth century, the significance of Cremona will ever remain of first magnitude in the story of the Violin.[3]

So writes Ernest Doring in the impressively titled *How Many Strads? Our Heritage From the Master; A Tribute to the Memory of a Great Genius, compiled in the year marking the Tercentenary of his birth; being a Tabulation of Works Believed to Survive Produced in Cremona by Antonio Stradivari, Between 1666 and 1737, including relevant data and mention of his two sons Francesco and Omobono.*

To return to the matter of "first magnitude" and ranking, it's no small mystery that this small town in the north of Italy should have provided the locus for so many of the world's important bowed wooden instruments. There are some who claim it was a function of the excellence of available timber, much of it shipped across the Adriatic; there are some who argue for the town apothecary and the varnish he produced; there are others who attribute this "genius of place" to the system of apprenticeship as such. Roughly between the latitudes of 44 and 46 degrees, from west of Milan to Venice and Udine (though the luthier David Tecchler lived in Rome and the Gagliano family in Naples), a group of craftsmen prospered. Andrea and Nicolo Amati, Francesco Ruggeri, and Andrea Guarneri were working in Cremona before Stradivari was born; Guarneri del Gesù, Carlo Bergonzi, Lorenzo Storioni, and G. B. Ceruti—this list is truncate, selective—continued after his death.

Most likely there is no single answer but a confluence of answers to the question: Why then and why there? The quality of wood and varnish, the nature of apprenticeship and exigencies of competition would each have played a role. But whatever the reason or reasons, in the seventeenth and eighteenth centuries a skill came to fruition in and near Cremona that has not been equaled since. Although genius itself may be neither explicable nor replicable, that part of the luthier's art which can be called pure craftsmanship can be in part transmitted—rather like the guild of stoneworkers, the Cosmati, who set the floors of churches and crypts with intricate inlaid geometrical patterns, then watched their trade die off.

This trade, however, thrives. More people play wooden stringed instruments more widely now than ever before; there's a flourishing business in both construction and repair. The membership directory of The American Federation of Violin and Bow Makers (1998–99) lists members from Ames to Zygmuntowicz with offices from Arizona to Wisconsin. René Morel's workshop in Manhattan contains no native English speaker but a polyglot transient or resident crew; his assistants speak Japanese, French, German, and Czech. Today the business is international, not local, and performers cross borders habitually; there's no fixed center of the music-making world. Yet the young luthier still travels to Cremona as a pilgrim to a holy place and, in the museum where the master's tools and patterns and drawings and instruments have been reassembled, still visits as though at a shrine.

For a few years the Cremonese were eclipsed: at the turn of the nineteenth century, German instruments outranked the Italians in terms of purchase price—but ever since then, in Jane Aus-

ten's phrase, "it is a truth universally acknowledged, that a single"
music lover "in possession of a good fortune must be in want of"
an instrument built in that time and place. And, if he or she be
very rich or skilled or fortunate, the instrument will likely come
from Stradivari himself.

*

"This is not my biggest restoration," says Morel. "I have done
much more difficult work than this, I have restored instruments that were considered garbage—when I was in my thirties
there was no challenge I wouldn't take. When I heard Maestro
Greenhouse play, while I was still at Wurlitzer, his sound always
moved me; it wasn't the largest sound, but whenever he touched
the string it was unforced. He is very much a perfectionist, very
much a serious person, the same way he is with his music—he
used to bring me the cello once a year to deal with the cracks
and all that, and he said, someday, René, you will work with this
cello and restore it entirely. And I said it would be an honor for
me one day to work for you. And now that he wants his cello
preserved, it is with this in mind that I am doing it. He's going
to get my best,"—the luthier spreads his hands and lifts his arms
and shoulders—"not the second best."

One of the major challenges has to do with varnish—worn
away since Stradivari's time and, inattentively, replaced. The
luthier shakes his head and points to blackened patches where,
he says, his predecessors took a housepainter's brush and went
slap, slap, drip. Morel removes these accretions with pure dena-
tured alcohol and a small sable retouching brush. Very carefully
he paints the alcohol across the grain with two, three, or four
strokes of the brush; he repeats this gesture often enough to
soften the surface of the varnish but not enough to go through,
then almost imperceptibly removes the loose new varnish with a
scraper or sharp knife.

To take off all such recent coating requires, self-evidently,
that Morel be able to distinguish between the varnish Stradivari

used and that which has been added since 1707. "It's not only the eyes," he tells me, "but also the feeling, the texture of the varnish, and the minute the original comes up you know that that is it." The varnish on the cello's back is almost wholly original, and so is the coloration of the scroll. But the varnish of the top had been much thickened and retouched, and when I ask him—pointing to an area of two square inches by the f-hole—how long it will take to clean this particular area to his own satisfaction, he says he cannot count how many days; it's one of the difficult jobs.

"Bernie says to me—I used to call him Mister Greenhouse, Maestro Greenhouse, but then he says, no, you must call me by the name my friends use, *Bernie*—make sure René you're the one to do this, because you have to know when to stop. If *you* put a drop of alcohol on that Strad varnish it will go to the white in no time, so you ask me, how can I use alcohol here? If *you* play the instrument and ask Bernie how much pressure do you put on the bow, he will raise his shoulders and shrug; if a virtuoso is going to play a concerto and he doesn't have the strings in tune, then he shouldn't attempt the concerto. I use alcohol, pure alcohol. And the answer to how to do it is skill. Skill, experience, feelings and concentration."

*

Windows line the workroom of Morel & Gradoux-Matt, Inc.; unshaded lamps increase the light. The room is narrow, high-ceilinged, and long; its shelves stock a jumble of shapes. Seventeen violins hang from a rack; there are dismembered instruments and cardboard boxes full of wood beneath the cluttered tables where the men bend to their work. They are in their twenties and thirties, convivial yet focused; they sport ponytails and paint-bespattered T-shirts and smell of resin, tobacco, and sweat. They rasp and sand and join and splice; they use clamps and calipers and scrapers and chisels and fine-pointed brushes and rags. There are boxes of spruce scraps, boxes of necks—labeled in black capital letters: CELLO, VIOLIN—a band saw, a poster of a Ferrari, cans of neck-graft, dental compound, rabbit glue, jam-jars labeled "chicory" and "potassium dichromate" with which they will varnish "white" wood. The radio plays. I expect to hear Haydn, Vivaldi perhaps—but what these craftsmen listen to is rock and roll, a D.J. selling cameras and Reeboks and reporting on the weather and traffic in New Jersey.

Morel walks through. He moves from desk to desk, assistant to assistant, examining their labors' progress, joking about masking tape and how I will steal his trade secrets. Half the work they do, he tells me, is to repair what had been badly done in other shops. When it looks very bad, he says, it's often not so serious, and when it's very serious it's not always easy to see. He points to a patch near an instrument's sound post, newly fitted and glued into place. Each cut begins with a saw in order, as Morel explains, "to approximate dimension. Then we use knives and rasps to remove most of the wood, and then we get the shape, and then after this we use files and in the end scrapers for very thin shavings. And then sandpaper, and after sandpaper we wet the wood three times, because when you wet the wood the grain rises, and it must be sanded back . . ."

*

Although the violin and violoncello have changed their shapes with time—in the former case a little, in the latter quite considerably—the pattern as such remains fixed. I mean by *pattern* the quintessence of form and not its surface adjustment; the cello's functional proportions were no doubt determined by trial and error, and that process continues today. Routinely someone claims to have discovered the "secret" of a Stradivarius and to reproduce its excellence in plastic or metal or by computer; routinely that someone is wrong. We may play electronic cellos, ergonomically friendly cellos, reduced or outsize cellos, but these are understood as variations on a theme. (The change in the structure of bows is a separate but related subject; the *beau idéal* of a Tourte bow stands in much the same relation to the run-of-the-mill version thereof as does a Stradivarius to a factory-issue machine.) And it's perhaps the case that contemporary instruments will "season" over time, sounding more impressive to the auditor in three hundred years. Still, the art and craft of the luthier attained its height in Cremona, and most modern practitioners attempt to imitate, not alter, that ideal.

It's as though Cézanne or Kandinsky sought only to paint in the manner of Titian or Brueghel, as though the contemporary writer tried only to write like the Greeks. For all practical purposes this fidelity to the ancient mode of instrument production remains the test of excellence, and I know no other métier of which this can be said. Singers, athletes, architects—each profits from the new technologies; they take advantage of modern techniques. The luthier too deploys special plastics, chemicals, calipers, and ultrasound for instrument repair. But the aim is reproduction, not innovation, and the model is a constant one.

To make such an instrument today would be to scale the heights of achievement; to equal that old mastery is the best that can be wished. Composers make new music, sculptors new sculpture, and carriage makers new cars—but a Stradivarius in private home or concert hall remains the practitioner's dream. For performer and audience both, in the nature of their handling or the volume and quality of sound produced, in terms of aesthetics or acoustics these wooden instruments have neither been improved upon nor by technology rendered obsolete.

Yet an instrument unplayed is an instrument ill-served. The use to which it must be put is audible, and over centuries such usage entails stress: material fatigue. It's not like a text which, printed, remains constant or a painting which, once framed, needs only to be seen. Fingers press on it; flesh brushes it; jewelry and liquor hover nearby, poised to scratch or spill; humidity alters from venue to venue and from day to day. The cellist who performs in Rio de Janeiro on Monday, in Seoul next week, and in London next month subjects his instrument as well as himself to continuous wear and tear. The glue will dry, the joinings split, the wood itself splinter, or the ornamental strips of purfling crack and the varnish fade. Inattentive or ignorant handling, a car crash or train wreck or water or fire: such threats are omnipresent and everything's at risk. Strings, bridges, end-pins, sound posts—each sooner or later requires attention and must be replaced.

*

Morel is a born raconteur, and he likes to tell stories of contests of skill; the style includes rodomontade. "I never had to work on commercial instruments. I had been trained in France, where my very first teacher was Marius Didier. He was seventy-two years old, and I was twelve years old, starting to make violins after school; later, in Mirecourt, I studied with *Maître* Amédée Dieudonné. So I developed skill for making violins in the old school of violin making, and in order to earn a living I had to make them at the rate of two violins—in the white, without varnish—per week. We had no machinery, not even an electric motor. And when I came to Wurlitzer I brought along my tools, and they came with the bandsaw, and I said, 'Well, you take your band-saw and I'll take my hand-saw and we'll see who finishes first. Also, who comes closer to the line, to the pattern.' We didn't bet any money, but I won; I won out over the band-saw. In my life as a luthier I seldom saw anybody else who could manage that way; it sounds as if I'm bragging but I'm not, it's a true fact.

"When I arrived at Mr. Wurlitzer and presented myself to Maestro Sacconi—this I will never forget—he gave me a bridge to cut, for a violin, a Lupot. Maestro Sacconi spoke French, and he said, 'This violin is one of your compatriots, and this is the model I want you to cut, that's the one I like.' So I gave him the new bridge maybe forty minutes later, and he said, 'Already?' And I said, 'Yes, why not?' So he looked at it, and I'll never forget his face, he said, 'My God!' Then he looked and looked and showed it to his right arm, D'Atilli; they couldn't believe that I'd cut it with my knife, you know, and they came to look at my knife because they couldn't believe that I'd done it with no knife marks, so clean and exactly similar to the model. The next bridge he gave me was for a cello, and after I'd cut that one he said, 'Bravo!'"

*

The cello is, of course, neither the first nor last wooden stringed instrument to have made its appearance in Europe; its ancestors include the lute and viol as well as the viola da gamba. Relatives include the violin, viola, and guitar. Its proper name suggests a "little violin," since *cello* in Italian is a diminutive, and the first such instrument clearly referred to in print—by Jambe de Fer in 1556—was a *"violoncello da spalla,"* which refers to the manner of holding the instrument in church processionals or serenades. *Spalla* means *shoulder* in Italian, and the player could perform while walking; the short-necked instrument was hung across the shoulder and fastened with a strap. By the turn of the twentieth century it had grown customary to abbreviate the name *violoncello* to *'cello* with the apostrophe indicating the six missing letters. By now it's acceptable to use the name *cello* without apostrophe and as a full designation; I have done so here.

This change in nomenclature suits the nature of such history; alteration inheres in the craft. Although the ideal of the instrument consists of intactness, no "pure" Stradivarius violoncello exists. There are roughly sixty still extant, and each differs from the cello as at first designed. No matter how earnest the performance of a practitioner of "early music," what the Maestro once heard in his workshop is not what we, listening, hear. What we look at is not what he saw.

A legend attaches to *"Le Messie,"* the Stradivarius violin in Oxford's Ashmolean Museum, that it was rarely if ever performed upon, and there are many instruments housed elsewhere under glass. This has the virtue of preservation—of keeping an artifact out of harm's way—but the luthier's work had been, of course, intended to be played. And if form follows function, then the form must shift.

In the seventeenth century the literature was written for
continuo (a bass-line repetition of the featured melody), but
Boccherini and Bach and their successors wrote for solo performance. This expansion of the repertoire and shift of emphasis
required an equivalent increase in acoustic volume and a heightened pitch. The neck was lengthened, the bridge raised, and the
fingerboard and interior bass-bar enlarged. In the nineteenth
century, traditional sheep-gut strings were wire-wrapped to aug-
ment the production of sound. The locus of recital also changed,
enlarging into concert hall, and an end-pin was added to provide
stability and anchor the frame to the floor. Today the violoncel-
list—unlike soloists on the violin, viola, or bass—must sit.

*

Here is Bernard Greenhouse on the first viewing of his instrument. It was not his first Stradivarius; he had previously owned
the "Visconti," a cello dated 1684 and in the "old pattern" (built
up from the viola da gamba). That instrument—now owned by
Mstislav Rostropovitch—had been "decorated," festooned with
the Visconti coat of arms in order to disguise its added wood.
The cello's sound, however, did not project well or merge com-
patibly with that produced by Daniel Guilet, the founding violinist of the Beaux Arts Trio. Therefore Greenhouse had been, as
he puts it, "in the market" and was in Europe on tour.

"In 1957, the instrument dealer, Jacques Français, said he
thought there might be a cello available near Cologne, in the
small city of Aachen, and that if I were ever in the neighborhood
I might just take a look. It happened that I was playing a concert
in Cologne, and we had a free afternoon, and so I took a train to
Aachen, which the French know as Aix-la-Chapelle. I arrived at
the station and looked in the telephone book for a *Geigenbauer*
[the German term for a luthier], then took a taxi to his shop and
told him I was an American cellist and had heard there was a
Stradivarius in the area: Did he know it and had he ever worked
on it? The *Geigenbauer*, Mr. Niessen, said by all means, yes. For

many years it had been in the collection of a Mr. Talbot, who had died just recently, and his wife still had the instrument . . .

"I asked him to call the daughter and find out if I might look at the cello; soon afterwards a man arrived, and I opened the cello case and fell immediately in love. I had no doubt, no doubt at all that it was a Stradivarius; I didn't even look inside to find the label. The color of the varnish, the shape of the instrument, it was so beautiful, so very beautiful, and it seemed to me a great jewel . . ."

How did the cello reach Aachen; where had it been before? It is now impossible to track the object throughout its lengthy provenance: who first commissioned or played it, how much it was valued and by whom. There would be charm and drama in such telling—witness the movie *The Red Violin,* where we see a fabled instrument in various cultural contexts, from Italy to China, and passing through various hands. That film may well have been inspired by John Hersey's novel *Antonietta,* in which the writer imagines a violin made by Stradivari while courting his second wife, Antonia Zambelli.

In both cases the dramatic problem is the same: How would this token of devotion be treated by musicians and collectors in the several centuries after having been created by a great luthier in love? In the film a nameless Cremonese mixes his dead darling's blood into the violin's varnish, and the instrument thereafter becomes an emblem of fatal romance. Hersey's plot is also episodic and sequential. He makes Mozart admire "Antonietta"; Berlioz and Stravinsky fall turn by turn under its spell, till it fetches up on Martha's Vineyard; thence the auction block . . .

Our information on the Countess of Stanlein's early history is limited yet suggestive. We know, for example, that "the late Count Stanlein" purchased it in 1854 from the French instrument maker and dealer, Jean-Baptiste Vuillaume (who was the foremost champion of Cremonese instruments in Paris at that time). Let's imagine for a moment that Count Stanlein (à la Stradivari in *Antonietta*) was courting a wife. He would have commissioned a string quartet or perhaps have been an amateur himself, so the name is his high compliment to their anticipated harmony: a nuptial gift of song. This was the period when chamber music, as the term indicates, was still a private matter; aristocrats routinely concertized at home. The Count's betrothed may well have sung or played the spinet, and he would have desired to join her in the music-room as well as in the bed. It's less likely, though possible, that the lady herself played the instrument, and that the Countess of Stanlein refers to the musician who held it between her spread legs. There's a tell-tale splash of brandy on the rear plate of the cello, where the varnish bubbled and was—perhaps by her handkerchief or the hem of a raised silk undergarment?—wiped clean.

Or perhaps Count Stanlein had no wife and fondled this substitute Countess instead. She would have been broad-beamed, deep-throated, her color reddish-gold. The instrument had previously been owned—witness the title "ex-Paganini"—by that notorious rakehell and virtuoso who sold it to Vuillaume. Vuillaume himself was a celebrated copyist; his gift of imitation remains unsurpassed, and he built many cellos on the model of the Countess—her proportions having been, by the mid-nineteenth century, acknowledged as ideal.

Here's what we do know of previous ownership, summarized dismissively by the brothers Hill in their *Antonio Stradivari, His Life & Work 1644–1737*. As historians of Stradivari, the Hill family—English dealers and instrument-makers—were, for many years, authoritative; their work remains fundamental to what is accepted today:

> The most interesting fact known to us concerning this instrument is the episode of its purchase early in the last century by Signor Merighi, a violoncellist of Milan, and Piatti's master. We have it on the authority both of Piatti and of Signor Pezze, also a pupil of Merighi, that in 1822, while the last-named was passing through the streets of Milan, he perceived a working man carrying, among other things, a violoncello

on a truck or barrow. Merighi at once accosted him and ended by becoming the owner of the instrument, which was in a dilapidated state, for a sum equivalent to 4s! Eventually, about 1834–35, Merighi disposed of the 'cello' to Paganini, who sold it to J. B. Vuillaume, who resold it in 1854 to the late Count Stanlein.[4]

In 1999 I visited the cello at regularly spaced intervals— January, March, May, June, August, October, November. It was rather like attending a much-loved patient in a nursing home or, more precisely, a hospital: the Countess of Stanlein lay broken, shattered, albeit on purpose, and then in surgery and traction and reconstruction, until little by little she was healed. On first view—broken down into component parts and contained in a stall in Morel's locked vault—the cello appeared as forlorn as it must have to Merighi in 1822. In the streets of Milan it had lain on a barrow; in the streets of Manhattan it stood in a bin, but only the trained witness would have thought it a thing of great value or envisioned the instrument whole.

*

In addition to work on the varnish, Morel had three principal tasks. The first involved a patch near the sound post top, which had been repaired before and unsuccessfully. The glue kept bleeding through minuscule cracks in the wood, and the luthier had to remove and replace what had been ineptly done—most probably in the mid-nineteenth century. The second and more complicated project was repair work on the ribs, which had been both wormholed and buttressed—sometimes to the thickness of 2.5 millimeters where Stradivari himself had carved to the thickness of 1.5. Morel must remove all the old glue and backing, then repair the damaged wood and steam the ribs again into their proper contours.

On 13 May 1999, for example, Morel takes a rib from its clamp. The wood had been in the clamp for five days, protected by padding and stretched to its original contour and its proper shape. There had been a doubling (a previous repair, with a second piece of wood glued on the inside), which Morel removes. The original width of the maple was 1.5 millimeters, and 0.3 millimeter of intact maple remains. Morel takes a new piece of unblemished wood and shapes it to the Stanlein rib, following the contour of the original exactly and attaching the two with glue. He lets the glue dry inside an airtight mold for two weeks. Then, removing it again, he reduces the width of the newly buttressed rib from 1.7 to 1.5 millimeters—thinning it down with a very sharp scraper to the desired thickness; smilingly he tells me, "You have to give it time."

An equivalent procedure holds true for the spruce top, which has bellied up and flattened out under the stress of the sound-post and strings; this warp from "true" contour might seem infinitesimal, but it is redressed. For this purpose the luthier constructs a plaster cast in order to determine where there were, as he put it, "bumps." The Stanlein top—delicately moistened in order to prove more malleable—is placed in a mold. All during the summer it lies encased in protective bindings beneath a sheet of brown paper so the wood itself will not be touched, and then a sheet of wax paper, and then a sack of hot sand.

At the same time, Morel has been refashioning the neck. The block into which the neck fits is a combination of three or four previous repairs, and where the neck joins the scroll someone has shaved a segment off the peg-box. This is a delicate job indeed, since the "original" wood at this junction is worn paper-thin. It has not cracked but is at risk. "I could have raised it with a bottom piece like it used to be at the turn of the century," Morel explains. Instead he puts a piece coming through from the inside out. A patch would have taken him two hours; this takes him two days.

"If you look here at the scroll,"—Morel points to its bottom edge—"originally, when Strad made the scroll, this part was not flat like this; there would have been a little step from the fingerboard, but by the time they changed the neck and fingerboard for

modern playing, you increase the angle. So they have been plan-
ing here. The curve should look like more like *this,* not flat"—he
finds a pencil-stub and draws the curve's arc on a piece of scrap
paper—"so if I angle it this way, it will be slightly below, which
is how it was done originally. It has been unscrupulously restored
before, but now we have respect for its value; so the original mor-
tise on the inside, the top-knot will start like this; I'm going to
leave four millimeters behind it, and here will come the fingerboard. If I did it the other way I would have to cut back some of
the original, and that I refuse to do . . ."

*

From 1707 to 1822, there's no formal record of the Countess of
Stanlein's ownership, and we can only guess at who played and
disposed of it how. The notion of a cello "on a truck or barrow,"
broken apart and ready for the municipal dump—then at the last
minute rescued by Merighi—has operatic flair. More probably
the thing was being trundled from one owner or shop to another;
most likely it wasn't defunct. But this did happen at a time, in
the wake of the Napoleonic Wars, when instruments were subject to rough handling. The "violin hunter" Luigi Tarisio—himself in large part responsible for the rediscovery of the Cremonese
masters—was said to have walked into Paris with his collection
in a sack. He had acquired his treasures in the north of Italy by
just such wayward and wayside encounter, finding instruments in
attics and church basements and the backs of barns.

So the Hill brothers' anecdote should be taken with a grain,
if not fistful, of salt. By contrast the certificate of authentic-
ity issued by the firm of Hamma & Co., Stuttgart, on 19 June
1949, rings with unstinting praise. From the Stanlein family the
cello would appear to have been sold to Albert Grümmer of the
Busch quartet, who sold it to the Talbots, from whom in turn
Greenhouse acquired it in 1958. The certificate has photographs
of the top, the back, and the scroll and then a description extol-
ling the virtues of the *"echt und zusammen-gehörend"* instrument,

the "*Violoncello mit Originalzettel, Antonius Stradiuarius Cremona 1707.*" That "dilapidated state" of which the Hills complain is gainsaid by the German firm, which writes: "In all its essential parts a very impressive Work of this Master; it is authentic and belongs together . . ."

Still, not all Stradivari's creations are equally achieved. They were fashioned by hand and piece by piece and with slight variations in wood and color and shape. Little adjustments of size and proportion loom large in terms of acoustics; some instruments are forgiving and mellow, others harsh and stern. From 1680 to 1700 the luthier produced at least thirty violoncellos, of which twenty-five survive, and they are without exception built of a large size (nearly thirty-two inches long, of an average, as opposed to twenty-nine and a half). Acoustically these instruments are an uneasy cross between bass viol and viola da gamba, and for seven years the workshop produced no documented cellos. Then the instruments emerged in the "great period"—a designation commonly attested to—from 1707 to 1720.

The Stanlein comes from the first year of this resumed production, and thereafter the pattern stayed fixed. The interval between 1700 and 1707 is therefore a telling time, and what we think of as the *ne plus ultra* of violoncello production lasted thirteen years. By 1720 the Master's hand began to shake or at any rate tremble a little and—with some exceptions—the work thereafter registers decline. His masterpieces of the great period include such other violoncellos as the Batta, the Castelbarco, the Davidov, the Duport, the Gore-Booth, and the Piatti. Often these were named for the aristocrats who commissioned or the musicians who performed on them, often for distinguishing characteristics—as in instruments called the *blonde* (referring to varnish color, since the characteristic Strad varnish of the period is a deep reddish-brown) and (his last violin) the "Swan."

Here, again, is Bernard Greenhouse speaking of his instrument: "The quality of sound is something that one wears, that adorns an individual as though it were a beautiful piece of apparel. The ear can be deceiving sometimes; sometimes I'll pick up one of the lovely modern celli in the morning and be very happy with it, but in the afternoon I'll ask what could possibly have pleased me. The ear changes; if you sneeze, for example, your hearing becomes clear and not pleasantly so; sometimes such a clarity is something you don't want. Sound is not absolutely fixed, not entirely a constant, but with my Strad there was never a time when I've been disappointed. No matter the weather or humidity, it stayed alive under my ear.

"There's a lusciousness about the sound. Under the ear it's a little bit coarse but this turns to velvet out in the hall, in the listener's ear. To the player there's an ease of performance no modern instrument can equal; the changes in the color of sound cannot be equaled. Color of sound is produced on an instrument in three manners; there are three elements to this, just as there are three primary colors in the painter's palette. We have the ability to place the bow closer to the bridge or to the fingerboard, and that produces a particular sound. In addition we have the speed of the bow, and the speed of the bow produces more sound without added pressure. That's the second primary color, and the third is the amount of effort we put into the bow. With those three primary colors we can produce an enormous variety of sound—analogous, again, to what a painter does with the palette."

*

And this is the heart of the matter, the core of the restorer's challenge. Since Greenhouse is completely pleased with the "palette" of the cello, any change in color must be by definition for the worse. It's not so much a question of leaving well enough alone as of separating out and protecting what cannot be improved. If the sound had been "lusciousness, velvet" before, how effect a restoration without risk?

The luthier is conscious of this issue and the exacting intensity of his client, and the two of them consult on what can and cannot be done. At some point, for instance (most probably in the late eighteenth century), a workman cut away a rear section of the scroll so as to gain easy access to the peg-wound strings. Morel could plausibly have filled in the wood and reconstructed the scroll—but this has become a "signature" feature of the cello, and the two men opted for consistency. Too, the brandy-spill that marred the varnish of the back has been reduced but retained; it's part of the Stanlein lore, and traces of that bubbling indiscretion—an admirer of Paganini perhaps, a hovering lover of the Countess?—have been kept.

The neck itself had been replaced since Stradivari's time, and therefore, though exact, the act of substitution need not have been exacting. The fingerboard glued to the neck is fashioned out of ebony; the wood of the neck is maple and—rubbed with oil rather than varnished—should be contrasted to the color of the instrument as such. In his country property Morel keeps a barn full of wood, and with barely concealed excitement he shows me a segment of old maple purchased in France some thirty years before: "Last weekend in the country I looked for pieces I might use and I found—discovered again, in my attic—a piece of wood from Vuillaume. It was cut quite thick and came from the stock of my grandfather's shop; my grandfather, at the turn of the century, was dealing in wood for all the violin makers of France. This piece is definitely from Vuillaume, because my grandfather stamped *his* wood with the initials PM; this was cut with a circular saw—you can see it on the grain, the *maille*—because they used hydraulic power and electricity had not yet been invented."

So the reconstructed neck brings this wheel full circle; in the mid-1800s Paganini sold the instrument to Jean-Baptiste Vuillaume, and at the turn of the millennium a French luthier restored it with wood from Vuillaume's private stock. What we have here—sent south from Paris to Marseilles, then shipped to New York and stored in an upstate barn until retrieved by Morel—is a piece of maple trimmed to shape and conjoined to an instrument built in Cremona: a constancy in change.

To restore the Stanlein so that it might seem brand-new would be to deny its history, and this has been the operational dynamic from the start. It's not unlike the problem posed by restoration of a famed work of visual art; Michelangelo's Sistine Ceiling—to take just one example—aroused disapproval when cleaned. A principal measure of any such instrument's value, indeed, is how much original varnish remains intact; there's a quasi-pietistic faith in the properties of Stradivari's "secret" formula as an ingredient of sound. Greenhouse remembers the excitement with which Fernando Sacconi informed him—on first encounter with the instrument—"There's enough varnish on this cello, original varnish, to have made three or four violins!"

So where Morel replaces the wood he imitates antiquity, replicating the grain of the spruce by brushstroke (having copied the "original" on tracing paper and transferring every capillary to the patch), then adding microscopic black spots as though the recent surface had darkened over time. He has tried to match the colors of the top and back, since the latter is almost unsullied and the former much retouched. To my eye—admittedly an amateur's—the finished product eradicates distinction and evades detection; only when he holds the wood to the light and a particular refractive angle, only when he points to it—"Here, Here!"—can I see where the "original" ends and its "imitation" begins.

*

The question of value is a complicated one; it too is subject to change. These instruments are rare enough to have no benchmark or average price, and this is truer of the cello—since there are so relatively few of them—than the violin. When an important van Gogh or Matisse routinely fetches tens of millions of dollars at auction, it's hard to escape the suspicion that a fine Strad remains undervalued. The 1727 Kreutzer Stradivarius (once owned by Rodolphe Kreutzer, for whom Beethoven wrote his Violin Sonata No. 9) was sold at auction in London for one-and-a-half million dollars in 1998; much more expensive purchases are prearranged and private. Experts agree or disagree; prices fluctuate from year to year and instrument to instrument—two, four, six million are being bruited now as sums—while the graph's curve points constantly up.

Consider this trajectory of purchase recorded by the Hills.

A violoncello dated 1730, the property of the Hon. Mr. Greaves, was offered for sale by auction at Messrs. Phillips. It was brought in, and subsequently sold in 1866 to W. E. Hill, who resold it for Ł230 to Mr. Frederick Pawle. Purchased back in 1877 for Ł380, and resold to Mr. Edward Hennell in 1878 for Ł500. Again repurchased in 1880 for Ł475, and sold a few months later to Mr. C. G. Meier for Ł525. The instrument now migrated to Paris, and was there bought in 1882 from MM. Gand & Bernardel *frères* for Ł600 by Mr. David Johnson, and brought back to England, to be once again purchased by our firm in 1885 for Ł650.[5]

Although these amounts now seem laughably small, it's important to note the celerity with which the instrument was purchased; only once did it register a small decline—of twenty-five pounds—and in the course of nineteen years its value nearly trebled. That exponential pattern of increase remains the case today. Stradivari produced only two known guitars and twelve violas, a few dozen celli but hundreds of violins, and value is of course proportionate to scarcity. While the law of supply and demand still obtains, the price will continue to grow.

*

The restoration had been estimated to take six months, but by March of 1999 it's clear that all hope of completion by summer will have been wishful thinking. As the months wear on, Morel begins to allocate his Saturdays and Sundays to the project; no phone rings in the weekend office, no customer approaches. When employed by Wurlitzer or Jacques Français, the luthier could ignore matters of administration and a balance sheet; now, as his own proprietor, he has to pay attention. Where once the work could be uninterrupted, there now are the issues of getting and spending, and his profit margin as a dealer is far larger than as a restorer. In the former instance the sums can reach hundreds of thousands of dollars, in the latter, tens, so his concentration is divided and his energy reduced.

"It may surprise you," he says, "but when I wake up at night I ask myself what I'm going to do, and then I make my plan. When I was young I'd make my plan, I'd tell myself I'm going to do this, this, *this,* and no matter how long it would take I would finish it; today if I do two-thirds of what I've planned I'm very pleased with myself, because my head is getting ahead of my physique. When I come home at the end of the day my eyes tear; I try to watch a little bit of the news and I can't even do that because it's very tiring. When you work all day with a magnifying glass it's very very tiring, because the focus shifts. For instance when I paint these grains here, I work very close, some-times so close that I cut the end of my brush because it touches my magnifying glass, but my hands are still steady, thank God. I keep saying if my eyes were as good as my hands I would still work like when I was thirty. But in this class of restoration it's the last one I can do . . ."

At eighty-four, Greenhouse had grown sleepless also. "Dur-ing many hours awake in the night," he says, "and even in my dreams I've thought about the instrument; when I first saw it in its dismantled form—lying on the bench in pieces—I stroked the ribs; almost as though it was a body, a living thing. I've traveled the world with that instrument; it's been my companion for forty years. It was my career, my *friend* . . .

"Of course I did have moments when I thought that, in this last period of my life, I could simply have had the pleasure of playing the instrument, of keeping it at hand. I have to fight to keep away from the telephone; my instinct is to call René every day and say, hey, did you do anything, has anything happened today? But each time I remind myself that things should be done to the instrument, they should have been done before my time,

and I thought I owed a debt to the cello. I thought that it had
done its service for me, I owed a service to it."

*

In fairy tales all things may be restored. That which disappeared
is found, and that which was hidden revealed. The crone transforms herself to princess when kissed by a sufficient prince; the
old grow young and fair and unblemished and supple once more.
To imagine the Countess of Stanlein first played is to people the
candlelit hall with an audience: stiff-backed gentlemen bewigged
and bright-eyed ladies whispering behind their fluttered fans.
The shade of Niccolo Paganini hovers nearby somewhere: elon-
gated, passionate, and bent above the bow. Or earlier—Merighi,
and those who came to visit the maker himself in Cremona—
the ones who came to purchase or to lodge an order or perhaps
apprentice to the trade. Who knows what Greenhouse dreamed
the day he shut his eyes and saw himself a youth once more,
agile, in the Pyrenees and learning from Casals?

In such a dream a cello floats upon the perfumed air. Ethe-
real, corporeal, it is the shape and very contour of encapsulated
sound. Its archings are perfectly rounded and smooth; its varnish gleams; the purfling lends a definition and a darkness to the
edge. From volute scroll to seamless rib the pattern of the wood
itself is intrinsicate with melody, suggestive of a promised pleni-
tude: yet resonant, yet mute.

On Tuesday, 23 May 2000, Greenhouse travels once more
to New York. Morel has spent the weekend readying the cello
for delivery—returning the strings he removed in 1998, making
adjustments to the sound-post and to his newly cut bridge. He
has prepared for this transfer carefully, stage-managing it to the
last detail: an impresario. It is eleven o'clock. The musician, arriving, palpably nervous, says, "I have dreamed of this moment, I
can't wait to see it, first I want to see it and then hold it and then
touch the bow to the strings. But before that I have to warm up."

Morel conducts him to a secondary office and produces a Stradivarius that was built with a flat back. "It's one of two Stradivari built where he tried out a flat back," he says. "But this one is cut down, its back is not original. You can buy it if you wish . . ." The sound of this cello is muted and nasal, but Greenhouse plays it nevertheless, tentative at first and elsewhere-focused; he is wondering, he tells me, if his own Strad's tone will have changed. "My fingers feel like sausages," he says.

After some time Morel reappears. "Are we ready, Maestro?"

In the large room at the atelier's rear there are signed photographs of Pablo Casals and Mischa Elman and Isaac Stern and photographs of Albert Einstein and Fritz Kreisler. Cello cases range like sentries at attention down the wall. Morel has placed a solid chair for the performer to sit on and, at the room's far end—some twenty feet distant, his back to the window—a second chair where he himself will listen in order to gauge projection. "All I did," he tells me, smiling, "was change the strings. It has taken me two years because I am very slow."

We laugh. Greenhouse is wearing glasses. Like a father with a newborn child or a husband with a long-lost bride, he receives the cello, embracing it, cradling it tenderly. He stares at the ribs, the front, the back, then turns the instrument upside down and reverses it again. He traces the edging, the purfling, the scroll. "Oh, René," he breathes. "It's beautiful. Bravo!"

At length he starts to play. He tries the open strings, tries fingerings, tries scales and then searches for "wolf" notes—the place where the cello's vibrations might clash and make the sound go flat and dull. Instead in the echoing space of this room the sound is pure, powerful, bright. "The *voice,*" says the musician, "it's just what I remember—what I've been hearing in my head. Exactly how she sang before . . ."

In a week or a month or a year, perhaps, Morel will make adjustments—but not now, not today. "There's nothing to adjust," the men agree.

Then there is lunch. This is a celebration, and we walk to a French restaurant in the neighborhood. Emmanuel Gradoux-

Matt joins the party, and the four of us order champagne. *"An die Musik,"* I offer, and Morel and Gradoux-Matt, clicking glasses, say, *"Santé,"* and Greenhouse says, "Chin-Chin." Close attention is paid to the menu and then to the prospect of food. "But the red wine with the entrée," cautions Morel. "They serve it too cold here. We should have the waiter bring it already. In this matter they are not quite correct. It has to be *chambrée."*

I ask my father-in-law. "What do you plan to do now?"

"I'm going to put my cello in its case and take a taxi to the airport and buy it a ticket and carry it home." Greenhouse raises his glass. "And we will never ever be separated again."

*

At 2:30 in the morning of Thursday, 1 June 2000, three cellists are fondling a scroll. The cello beneath it stands mute. "Sensuous," says Yo-Yo Ma; "Sensational," says Ko Iwasaki. Bernard Greenhouse, its owner, traces the instrument's neck. "Sensuous," says Ma again, and smiles and shuts his eyes.

This has been a long day. The week-long World Cello Congress III is taking place in Towson, Maryland, and more than five hundred cellists flock to master classes and panels and recitals both exhaustive and exhausting. Wednesday's program, for example, has included a symposium, "Influence of Folk Music on Cello Literature," a discussion of Cello Music from China, Music on Jewish Themes, a workshop on Jazz Improvisation, a film, a master-class taught collectively by Janos Starker, the Honorary President of the Congress, and Greenhouse, its Artistic Advisor.

The evening's concert, in Meyerhoff Symphony Hall, has featured two young musicians, Wendy Warner—in her twenties—and the teen-aged Han-Na Chang. After intermission, and to thunderous applause, Yo-Yo Ma and the Baltimore Symphony Orchestra perform a new composition, "The Six Realms" by Peter Lieberson, and Tchaikovsky's "Andante Cantabile Op. 11." Then comes the usual postconcert line of well-wishers and then a bus-trip for invited guests to a reception on a cruise ship in the harbor. The bus driver, however, gets lost; the ship proves difficult to find, tucked into a dark corner of the marina, and by the time the cruise begins it is well past midnight. Dutifully, drinking jug-wine and decaffeinated coffee, the cellists and their sponsors make slow circles in the harbor while the engines thrum and mutter and the lights over Baltimore dim.

On the bus-trip back to Towson University, where the artists have been lodged, Greenhouse invites Yo-Yo Ma to look at the cello. Ma is gracious and respectful and, it seems, indefatigable; the night before he had been visiting late with Starker; in a few hours he must leave for New York. But this cello commands his attention, and he and Ko Iwasaki appear in Greenhouse's suite. Ma carries his tailcoat over his arm; his dress-shirt and black tie seem casual now, and he's sweating lightly in the late spring heat. With a flourish, unlocking its case, the elder man produces his reclaimed "Paganini Strad."

"Beautiful," says Ma.

"Sensational," Kawasaki repeats.

"Here." Greenhouse proffers a bow.

The virtuoso demurs. Shaking his head, eyes narrowed behind wire-rimmed glasses, Ma studies the cello front and back, then plucks the strings and commences to play pizzicato. Kawasaki claps. After some time Ma takes the bow and—"Noodle a little," Greenhouse urges—plays a few notes lightly, dreamily, so as not to wake the sleeping guests. I ask him what he's hunting, what he listens for, and he says: the things it's easy to do, the things that are hard. It is three o'clock by now, and the men forget their resolution to be circumspect. "You should *hear* it," Greenhouse says. "Full-throated, down by the bridge."

Iwasaki excuses himself and collects his own cello, then returns to the room. He too possesses a Strad, dated 1727, but this is a copy of the one he left at home—one of six made by a luthier up in Michigan—and the men measure proportion, dimension, comparing instruments. They talk of other cellos, other makers, other performers. What they do not talk about is price. Yo-Yo

Ma keeps caressing the Stanlein's scroll, and when I ask him what the word is for what this instrument possesses he says, *"Gravitas."*

*

At the conference on Thursday morning Morel gives a speech, discussing the technique of instrument making and repair, its challenges, its history. "I believe a lecture should be like a woman's skirt," he jokes. "Long enough to cover the subject, short enough to keep it interesting." The audience laughs. Then he discourses on the physics of sound, the general problems of restoration, and "Cello Making for Today's Virtuoso."

Each day in the hotel suite, Greenhouse and Morel have been "fiddling" with the Stanlein's sound-post, shifting its position so as to apply greater or less pressure to the top. Since he wants a set-up with which he is familiar, Greenhouse shifts bridges also—first trying the original Sacconi bridge, then the one Martin Cornellisen cut for his own copy of the instrument. "It doesn't fit," protests the luthier. "You can put a dime under its feet. It's a good bridge, I'm not saying anything against the bridge—but not for this cello," he says

Greenhouse is unconvinced. "The strings sit too high with the one that you cut for me. You listen to it in this room, your ears are excellent, of course, I trust them absolutely, but *I'm* the one who plays. And it's too hard with this bridge."

"But that will change," Morel repeats. "The top has been lying alone for a year and a half; it will need to be adjusted. A month from now, *Maître,* you bring it back to the shop. And then"—he spreads his hands—"we will see what we hear."

What they see and hear in Meyerhoff Symphony Hall is the refurbished instrument, its sound resplendent now. As Greenhouse comes onstage, two hundred cellists stamp their feet in a drumroll of appreciation for their "artistic adviser." This will be his first appearance in the full space of the concert hall, the first time the cello "sounds out." He plays the solo in "Song of the Birds"—a Catalan folk-song transcribed for the cello by Pablo

Casals. "I have performed it," the musician says his teacher told him, "hundreds, hundreds of times."

It's a simple melody, an evocation of birdcalls and flight, an easy line to play and difficult to master. This is mastery. Greenhouse has his eyes half-shut, his old head bending heavily, his feet and hands and body engaged, his cello in his arms. Behind him rank upon rank of cellists listen and respond. "There were tears in our eyes," says Luis Claret, himself a Catalan. "There were many of us crying."

The audience erupts. Greenhouse rises, bows, accepts flowers. "He has moved beyond music," the man to my left, standing, says.

N.B. This essay appeared in *Harper's Magazine,* January 2001, with the subtitle "Sound and Soundness in a Stradivarius Violoncello." It was reprinted in *The Best American Essays 2002* (ed. Stephen Jay Gould) and also—enlarged, illustrated, and rearranged—as a book titled *The Countess of Stanlein Restored: A History of the Countess of Stanlein, ex-Paganini Stradivarius Violoncello of 1707* (London: Verso Press, 2001).

Bernard Greenhouse died at home in Wellfleet, Massachusetts, at the age of ninety-five. Nearly eleven years after the concluding scene of this essay, at life's end he slept with "The Countess" beside him in his bed. René Morel too died in 2011, at the age of seventy-nine. In order to settle the cellist's estate, and to comply with his wish that it be heard in performance, the instrument was sold in 2012.

As part of additional research undertaken during the process of bringing the cello to market, we learned that the proper spelling of a previous owner should have been Stainlein, not Stanlein, and that the Count was himself an avid composer and musician. The dealer Christopher Reuning, of Boston, made a convincing case that the Countess was part of the Paganini Quartet (four Stradivarius instruments owned by the famed violinist) and the very model of the "Forma-A" template Stradivari produced in 1707, the year he codified the cello's present shape. I have chosen not to make such additions or corrections but to reprint the article in its original form. A very few word changes have been made, but the *Harper's* article is otherwise intact.

As the press was avid to report, the instrument sold at private auction (to a Canadian foundation); part of the sales agreement was that the price be undisclosed. It is, however, a record sum for a violoncello and has yet to be surpassed. The Countess today is on loan by the foundation to a young Canadian cellist, Stephane Tetrault, who will play it for the foreseeable future. There are, in other words, things to add and alter in the story of the cello's life, and that life goes on.

Endnotes

1. Henry W. Hill, Arthur F. Hill, and Alfred E. Hill, *Antonio Stradivari, His Life & Work (1644–1737)* (New York: Dover Publications, 1963; unabridged republication of original volume, London: W. E. Hill & Sons, 1902), p. 20.

2. This description derives from Elizabeth Cowling, *The Cello* (New York: Charles Scribner's Sons, 1975), pp. 17–19.

3. Ernest Doring, *How Many Strads: Our Heritage From the Master; A Tribute to the Memory of a Great Genius, compiled in the year marking the Tercentenary of his birth; being a Tabulation of Works Believed to Survive Produced in Cremona by Antonio Stradivari, Between 1666 and 1737, including relevant data and mention of his two sons Francesco and Omobono* (Chicago: William Lewis & Son, 1945), pp. 20–21.

4. Hill, op. cit, p. 132.

5. Ibid., p. 273.

A Visit to the Gallery

The most popular cultural attraction in New York is the Metropolitan Museum of Art; almost seven million people visit its buildings each year. Tourist groups fly to Bilbao for the sole purpose of a trip to Frank Gehry's Guggenheim; others, with a similar intention, travel to Paris or Kyoto or Dubai. Every month in China, or so it seems, a new museum breaks ground. For the contemporary architect, these structures are major commissions, for the major collector, prime sites. There is widespread interest in such edifices now, and beyond the commercial aspect of this market phenomenon we bring a leaven of reverence: *museo,* the place of the muse.

All my life I have approached that thing called a *museum* as something special, hallowed. By this I do not mean that no sound is welcome and no school group should visit—but the hush of expectation and attentive searching does have in it somehow a component of worship. We make, I think, a pilgrimage within a sacred grove. We enter a museum building in a way that differs from the way we enter, say, an office building or shop (though a museum may contain those latter spaces as well).

Why, I wonder: What sets it apart? And should it in fact be separate or, as others suggest, folded seamlessly into the fabric of society? Does it best serve its purpose as a kind of sanctum, even sanctuary, or as a part of the whole? My reflections on these questions are a privacy made public—not a bad working definition of the function of display-space—and an attempt to answer or at least ask why such a place should matter and what it represents.

*

My parents were both refugees from Hitler's Germany who knew each other glancingly; later they reunited in London. I was born there during the Second World War and came to this country when young. As "Delbanco" suggests, my father's people took their name in Italy, but they left Venice as long ago as 1630 and had been living in Germany for three hundred years. Both families were prosperous—bankers and businessmen—the sort of *bürgerliche* Jews who couldn't quite accept that Hitler might mean them. Albert Speer, his architect, worked on my maternal grandparents' house in Berlin; Karl Schmidt-Rotluff fashioned jewelry for my father's mother in Hamburg. I don't mean to overstate the case; they weren't major players in the world of art, but it was always understood to be of consequence, to *count.*

This was the sort of culture in which oil portraits were commissioned, in-house concerts offered of a Sunday after lunch, and wood furniture polished to a fare-thee-well by the upstairs maid. They were supporters of the Bauhaus, collectors of German Expressionist paintings and—more surprisingly, since this was very early on—tribal objects and African masks; my father had, *has* an eye. My first memories of life with him have much to do with museums; he was an inveterate—even an obsessive—visitor.

No sooner did we reach a town than we were off to see the artwork it was famous for, and he did *know* a town in terms of what was hanging there, or which square contained what Donatello sculpture it was important to see. He read few books; he had trouble remembering people's names; he had no difficulty whatsoever recalling the Goya on the southwest wall of the upstairs space he'd visited in Madrid in 1928. He's ninety-seven now and this remains the case; he will forget what happened yesterday but not the composition of a Kirchner or Degas he saw eighty years before . . .

In my early childhood I had small volition; I simply assumed it was what people did and how they viewed the world. Later, when the age of anxiety set in—which is to say, when I first learned to be embarrassed by my parents—I can remember protesting, *Do we have to, can't we stay in the hotel, can we eat something first at least?*—while he set off, his sons in tow, to the Duomo or Uffizi or Accademia or Louvre or some less trafficked building or church whose guardian was just about to shut the doors when this importunate person approached. In those days the lighting was quite often dim, controlled by some custodian or monk who dozed beside the switch; always my father would walk up to him, a fistful of lire or francs outstretched. I would stand as far away as possible, in an agony of discomfiture, but the bribe did work and the lights went on, and, presto, Masaccio or Matthias der Mahler appeared.

Other children spent time with their fathers playing baseball or fishing or working on cars. I spent Saturday mornings at his side, painting or sitting for portraits, because he was a more than Sunday painter and an accomplished one. Several of his portraits are in fact in public places—the National Portrait Gallery, Harvard College, the Museum of the City of New York. He never quite had the daring or drive to make a career of it and was a collector more than a creator. But he had genuine talent and does love to draw and still, in his great old age, declares, "A painting a day keeps the doctor away." When he came home from a business trip it was always with something acquired en route: a Zuni Bowl or hermaphroditic standing figure with breasts and penis. I'd stare at in wonder, an etching by Rembrandt or woodcut by Dürer or poster by his favorite, Henri Toulouse de Lautrec. Lautrec's Aristide Bruant turned his broad back above my childhood bed; Yvette Guilbert smiled soulfully down; La Goulue lifted her leg. There were oil paintings in the dining room by Lovis Corinth and Chagall. And always, when we traveled, it was to the museum or the monastery or the chapel at the edge of town my father took us first.

My mother went along with it; she didn't have much choice. She drew the line, however, at his absent-minded tardiness; he was habitually late and she—no doubt in compensation—was a close clock-watcher, always prompt. "Punctuality," she used to say, "is the politeness of Kings." "Just a minute, just a minute," was his mantra, and he'd peer all the more fixedly at the mask or cabinet of curiosities or jade blade that had arrested his gaze. Once, I remember, when we first traveled in America and had tickets on a train called the 20th Century Limited passing through Chicago, there was time enough prior to boarding to visit the Art Institute; we left the station and took a taxi to the museum in order, as he told us, to pay our respects to Seurat. Pointillism is a painstaking technique, and everything about those Sunday morning strollers on La Grande Jatte argues leisure, so I suppose it was inevitable that we got back to the station as the train was pulling out. We made it, in fact; we did board. But all these decades later, when I walk up the steps to what the locals call the *toot,* I hear that train whistle blowing and break out into a sweat.

*

My uncle too took me along, though he was a genuine expert and—that daunting word—*connoisseur.* As a student of art history my father's older brother had earned a doctorate for his dissertation on Abraham Bloemart; in prewar London he established—along with two equally knowledgeable partners—a gallery in Old Master paintings and prints. Later, the partners went "modern"—or, anyway, as far as Walter Sickert and Auguste Rodin. An early memory, for me, and a source of unending if childish delight, was the game we'd play together. We'd enter a room of a museum—and sometimes, to my certain knowledge, one he hadn't visited before. Then I'd run up to a canvas or a piece of statuary and, having read the attribution and blocked it with my reaching fist, would ask my uncle who'd produced it when.

He was never wrong. He always got it right. He knew, it seemed to me, everything, every single artist's name, and if the attribution was to that greatest of all creators, Mr. or Ms. Anon, he'd know the country and the century of provenance instead. When I asked him how he did it, he said *handwriting*: he could read an artist's pen- or brush-stroke as though the name were signed.

His gallery was a brick four-story Queen Anne townhouse just off Bond Street and the Burlington Arcade. After college I spent time there, with the not-so-hidden expectation that it might become a way of life and art-dealing my profession. I was at loose ends, a little, trying to decide if England might be home again and—since I loved my uncle—happy to work at his side. It was an education. I followed him to Christie's and to Sotheby's, to country homes and The Royal Academy, to the studios of painters, sculptors, frame-makers, restorers; I watched while he authenticated, or refused to, the name on a canvas or named it if unsigned. I learned much. But soon enough I also learned that selling other people's art was not my chosen path.

If someone appeared near the desk where I sat, I'd say, "Good morning, sir." Then one of my uncle's partners—the one concerned with social niceties—informed me that what I thought common politeness was inappropriate and might be construed as, in fact, *common* politeness. The chap who brought my tea would say, "Good morning, sir," but *I* shouldn't do so to a customer, since it suggested I was of an inferior social position. Unless of course he *was* a sir, in which case I should say, "Good morning, Sir Richard, Sir John . . ."

I learned the proper way to address a lady born to a title or a lady married to it—the distinction between Lady Jane and Lady Addison; I learned that the seedy, ill-shaved, threadbare fellow skulking by the stairwell was either a thief or an Earl. And after a few months I found that I could no longer be happy in London; its world was not my world. One day my uncle took me aside and said, "This isn't working, is it; you're arriving in the gallery later and later each morning, you leave as soon as you can. Why don't we admit it; this isn't for you; get out of here and write . . ."

That is the self-congratulatory version of the story, the one where our young hero espouses democratic principles and renounces the world of privilege and private dealing in favor of his own and sullen art. The other version—truer—is that I never knew enough about the field to make a go of it, and wasn't willing to study. Week after month my uncle and I would walk into a room together; he'd know every painting there and I'd know that my feet were wet or that the girl in the corner wasn't wearing a brassiere or that in twenty minutes I could propose we have lunch. Sometimes, still, I think of it—the road not taken, the life unlived—and wonder what would have happened if my uncle and his partners had been a little more invested in, as it were, the succession; I might have stayed in London or opened a dealership branch in New York. Then, instead of John Q. Public and an interested amateur, I might have been professional and full of earned learned opinion and, like my uncle, a crank.

The last time he came to America, he visited my family; he was in his nineties, and in short order would die. As is the case with my father, a trip to see us in Ann Arbor always included a visit to the Detroit Institute of Arts and the museum in Toledo. He'd sold them both some paintings and liked to visit with, as he put it, his "old friends." On the final day I took him to the University of Michigan's Museum of Art—which was displaying, with a certain amount of fanfare, a terra cotta warrior and horse from the Han dynasty. These had arrived from Toronto and were being readied for an exhibition which the sponsors claimed—with justification, I suppose—would be the first showing of these newly discovered artifacts in the fifty states.

My uncle approached, was introduced, and asked if he might offer an opinion for the press. I remember his response. "One of the advantages of great old age," he said, "is that we need not be respectful of the merely ancient. From an anthropological point-of-view these objects have some value. But from an *artistic* stand-point, they are of course only rubbish." Then, leaning on his cane, he limped away to view the Max Beckman painting—*Begin the Beguine*—that he loved.

Beckman's work is highly referential, or so it seems to me: full of signs and symbols and gestures to personal history. My uncle knew Beckman a little, had visited the artist in St. Louis and asked him at some point about the meaning of some image emerging on the easel before which they both stood. The par-rot or the crutch or the black bow-tie or whatever it was that had piqued the dealer's interest fairly begged for explanation. The painter declined to explain. Pressed, he refused to again. Finally he said—a warning-shot across the bows for anyone who talks or writes of art—that the picture must speak for itself. "I *never* talk about my work," he said. "*Niemals.* What's here is here. Enough."

*

In London, during the Second World War, such silence was put to the test. For good and sufficient reason, the treasures amassed in museums were dispersed and hidden in the countryside, since a single direct hit by Hitler's *Luftwaffe* on, say, the National Gallery of Art or the British Museum would have been a catas-trophe. But Kenneth Clark—the man I would learn to call *Sir* Kenneth—proposed that they risk one painting or sculpture a month.

This became known as "Picture of the Month" and was placed on brave solo display in the National Gallery. By all accounts it mattered hugely: Londoners on their lunch-break or with that special, single work in mind fairly streamed into the museum and were uplifted and consoled by Raphael or Ingres or whoever had been chosen as a potential sacrifice. (Wanda Landowska did much the same, giving concerts in the gallery and comforting her audience with the piano music of Bach.) So I think of the place of the muses in that emblematic instance: it must have offered up some sense of lastingness, of focused attention on what has endured. The *museo* was making a hopeful assertion: this misery also will pass. It strengthened for the present and emboldened for the future those who stood in front of what had gone before.

Today we call it a "Blockbuster Exhibition." Today it's "Have you been to the **A** or **B** or **C** at **X** or **Y** or **Z**"—fill in the blanks. The experience of seeing includes the act of being seen—to have been part of a multitude and made, as it were, "the scene." There's nothing wrong with this; it's collective witnessing and it has its yield. The theater, for example, is more powerful and, in the case of comedy, *fun* when there are others beside you and the room is full. But this member of the public prefers to go alone—or with a friend or loved one in the family. I like rooms better empty, and best in near-total silence. Because in the end that's always why I enter a museum—as though for this month's masterpiece, the chance of solitary contemplation in the midst of threatful war . . .

Think of Michelangelo in the Vatican or the Rothko chapel in Houston or the Rivera in Detroit: three very different representations of reality and pictorial homage to the sublime. Each offers a sustained encounter with a single artist's work. Surely most of us, if given the chance, would choose the uncluttered room and focused vision, no matter how "busy" a canvas or fresco greets us from ceiling and wall. In some cases, indeed, there's crowd control enforced in order to preserve the masterpiece at risk. The caves of Lascaux, for instance, or da Vinci's restored *Last Supper* in Milan can be looked at or breathed on only by limited numbers of folk at a time, and when you pass through those air chambers and sealed doors, you have precisely that sense of earned difficult access: a formal, measured, slow approach, and then a goal attained.

But there's another kind of installation which museums also traffic in: the jumble, the exuberance, the cornucopia displayed. Let's call this the Pitti Palace Principle, where more paintings occupy a space than anyone can plausibly see or absorb; often they're hanging far up by the ceiling and always cheek by jowl.

It's the obverse of the notion of a reverential progress towards a waiting icon; it's meant to dazzle, to cow. And it does. It says to us mere mortals that here is a godly abundance, superabundance, the museum as storehouse and warehouse of art. The room is full to overflowing, not reduced to its essential, and the very language that I'm using to describe it partakes of just such excess: *cornucopia, abundance, superabundance, storehouse, warehouse, cheek by jowl.* This goes, I think, some distance to explaining why "a visit to the gallery" is often so demanding, a kind of sensory overload it's hard to sustain over time. And most museum goers wilt under the barrage. For we feel weary, puny, reminded of inconsequence—"Hast *thou* created Leviathan?" as the voice in the whirlwind asks Job.

A final reference to my uncle, and I'll let him rest in peace. One of the paintings in his living room was an important early Rubens, an oil he had discovered in an estate sale somewhere when that sort of thing was still possible in England. He bought it in the 1950s and kept it for most of his life. It's an energetic canvas—*The Fall of Phaeton*—full of prowess and youthful exuberance, the young genius taking a subject and proving how much he could do. There are horses, clouds, the sun-shot sky, a chariot, the radiant muscularity of an overreaching hero soon to die.

The painting hangs now in our own National Gallery, in the nation's capital, and I visit it each time I go to Washington. It's a bittersweet encounter and a long shared history that, when I approach it, revives. There's the smell of cigars, of cigarettes, of chocolate and schnapps and tea being poured; there's my childhood, then young manhood, the desultory chit-chat of the elders of the tribe. Most likely they're speaking in German; there's music and roses and chess. Somewhere there's a whiff of turpentine and linseed oil, somewhere Chanel #5. I've known this canvas all my life, leaned up against it often. But if I dared to touch the thing, the bells would no doubt whistle and a guard approach.

So possibly that too is what we find in museums: this thing I've called a privacy made public. Or call it an intimate distance, an ownership by adjacency—for I don't think it matters much that long ago and far away this particular Peter Paul Rubens hung in my uncle's house. Each of us can own a painting by looking hard and often enough; each of us can make it part of our personal history and, by extension, our family's lore. Ideally, and by extension, we each own it all.

*

Here, a brief digression and pet peeve. It's not an accident that I've been referring to the National Gallery in London, or the University of Michigan Museum in Ann Arbor, or our National Gallery in Washington. One of the things they have in common is that admission is free. I'm not consciously a skinflint and don't mind paying for a sports event or concert or the like. And I of course do understand how important to the operating budget of an institution is the price of entry, as well as the sense of value attached to something we pay to receive. If it costs ten or twelve—or, more recently, twenty-five—dollars it must be worth it, we say. But you don't have to be a tightwad to bridle at the cost of just ducking into a show or casting a quick glance around at the day's display. Sure, one can become a member; sure, museums are expensive to maintain. But I believe that something important is added to the experience of viewing when we know that everyone who wants to can afford it, and something important gets lost when turnstiles bar the door. For I'm not sure, says John Q. Public, that penny-wise isn't pound-foolish; museum attendance is going up, yes, but it might have done so exponentially if it weren't such an investment to attend. There's a very special sense down in our nation's capital or in university collections or the few private museums so well endowed that entry *is* free—a sense of collective ownership. I think it worth much more than ten or twenty dollars per visit to signal to the passerby: our gate is unlocked. Do come in.

*

My wife is a painter, and a first-rate one, though she's far too modest to call herself professional. Which is to say, she makes her paintings for pleasure—often, the pleasure of others—but not for the profit as such. In that sense she's an amateur, a lover of the enterprise, and while she's at the easel she's entirely focused, completely engaged. Lately I've found myself watching the way she watches the world, in particular its colors. Robert Graves, writing of writing, called that secondary set of eyes "The Reader over Your Shoulder"; in this case it's "The Viewer," and I try to see what she is seeing as, long years before, I tried to look the way my father or my uncle looked at what they made or bought and sold.

This is, I think, another thing that happens in museums: the emphasis on and the primacy of eyes. Self-evidently, in a symphony hall, what matters are our ears, in a restaurant our taste buds, and so on and so forth; the sense engaged the instant we enter a gallery is the sense of sight. There's much we glance at or gloss over in the daily round, much we don't look closely at or fail to scrutinize. But the faculty of vision—what we see and how we see it—is essential, *quint*essential to this particular world.

There are certain rooms in a museum where painters set up shop and copy what's already there—taking someone else's work and more or less minutely replicating it. It's fine to see them looking and watch others watching while they do: a set of concentric circles, really, radiating outward from what the painter saw. Like those self-portraits of an artist in his studio, surrounded by his collection and wares: a kind of advertisement that's not so much a *trompe l'oeil* as a trumpeting of what can be seen when studied closely and with a view to imitation. Much art in this regard is variation on a theme, and some of the most interesting shows I've seen in the last years acknowledge this fact and stress it— placing Manet and Velazquez side by side together, or Picasso and Matisse. To see as others saw, to look over the shoulders of

Turner or Homer or Ruysdael, is in an almost literal sense to enlarge our vision and render sight acute.

The reader will perhaps have noticed that I've named a lot of names; this visit to the gallery is consciously a survey and a rapid tour. (In that regard, I've avoided the principle of "Picture of the Month" and entered the Pitti Palace instead, intending to ramble, not pause.) Any true painting enhances alertness and rewards repeated viewing; we see it first in its entirety and then in its component parts—the reverse of our procedure with a symphony or novel, which we cannot hear on the instant or deal with except over time. Any true artist deserves extended attention, of course, and a look at more than one example of her or his craft. That's the point of exhibitions and the purpose of collecting in a focused way.

But one of the pleasures of museum-going is a canter through the field of art, the gift of covered ground. Where else can you move from France to Korea, from England to the Congo, and Italy to India at such an easy clip? And since this is a surface-scratch—necessarily constrained by time and space—it may suffice to say that museums also offer a chance to see the world. Take it while you still can manage, urges my father; take it, repeats the ghost of my uncle; take it, I tell myself now. Not all of us are fortunate enough to travel unimpeded, but all of us can enter the storehouse, the warehouse of culture—and map out terrain on the walls.

*

I began this essay with family stories, and I want to close with one more. My maternal grandparents knew enough to leave Berlin for Paris as the Third Reich grew more threatful, though they left much behind. One of the things they took with them was a small oil painting by one of the six "founders" of Impressionism, Alfred Sisley. It's a beautiful canvas and a well-documented one—a boat hauled up on the shingle, in an open-air dry dock: *Bateaux en Réparation à St.-Mammes* (*Boats under Repair at Saint-*

Mammes). It has Sisley's signature water, beach, and sky; it's brilliantly composed and colorful—a kind of motion in stasis they carried with them, I suppose, as an emblem of what might be saved. When it came time to flee Paris, they entrusted the oil to a friend. It's a long and complicated history, with dealers' names like Cassirer and Durand-Ruel involved, with the thing hidden in an attic in the environs of Vichy and then somehow sent to New York and L.A. and just now fetching up for sale at Sotheby's in Manhattan.

I know about this because my grandfather did lodge a claim, as long ago as 1950, with the German government for reparation for confiscated art and household goods. And there are organizations that help with the recovery effort and are superbly competent at research; I know, for example, the train my grandparents attempted to take out of Paris, the date they were turned back, and the date they succeeded in leaving; I know which camps they were interned in and when they were released. I know who attested to having seen the painting where, and the given names and middle names and surnames of those through whose hands it has passed. I know who claimed to own it and what the claims consist of and how—via the Art Loss Register—they have been disproved. A cousin has a lawyer and the lawyer stopped the sale; soon enough, perhaps, we'll know to whom the Sisley now belongs.

To me, of course, this story has significance—of both an emotional and fiscal kind. I think of that canvas, *Boats under Repair at Saint-Mammes,* and see the boats they—we—managed to travel on to this brave new world. But it's a very different tale from the one about Peter Paul Rubens, and even if the Sisley ends in a museum, it will not be a privacy made public in quite the same way. I never saw that particular painting hang on a family wall.

Rather, it's the trail of tears that many artifacts from many different cultures have been transported along—the shard of pottery from Arizona or bronze totem from Benin, the manuscript from Baghdad or piece of decorated rubble from what was once

Bamiyan. All things that hang or stand in a museum collection were—it's the appropriate word—*appropriated* and sooner or later installed somewhere else. It's just as true of obelisks or the stones of leveled monasteries as of a canvas spirited out of the country in what became a lost suitcase; transport in its doubled sense is a necessary function of both the collector's impulse and the curatorial task. Here the exemplary instance is perhaps the Elgin Marbles: one culture arrogating the treasures of another and putting them out on display.

In that sense, as we've increasingly come to see, the story of museums is a complicated back-and-forth of provenance and preservation, of empire and acquisition, a playing out of the old adage that to the victors belong the spoils. We've traveled a long way by now from my early memories of monks nodding at the light switch while my father bribed them to turn on the light, but it's the same road, really: one person standing rapt in front of what another made. The linkage may be near or distant; the connection may be difficult to prove. But it is, I think, another reason that museums matter and we're in a sacred grove; in the end the way a painting comes to hang upon a wall—for what reason it was painted, by whom, when, where, who first commissioned or purchased it, who commandeered or stole it—is useful only as narrative and a kind of factual embroidery. What's here is here. Enough.

Curiouser and Curiouser

Curious George and the Pair Who Conceived Him: H. A. & Margret Rey

```
Dear Mr. H. A. Rey
I like monkeys because they eat bananas every
day. I am sure they eat bananas every day.
Your friend, Stephanie G.
```

*

Let us imagine our hero full-blown, although his gestation was slow. From the first we loved Curious George. He does not speak; he cannot speak; he will not formulate words. Yet his emotions and actions have an intrinsic eloquence: we know what he is thinking, what he delights in or fears. In animated versions everywhere on-screen today, the chattering creature makes himself clear; *Hoo-hoo, ha-ha* suffices as speech. The mouth turns up, the mouth turns down; we *know*. In retrospect it seems he's always been a member of the family; when George does get in trouble, his predicaments are ours.

And more and more, it seems, his behavior is familiar. He ponders, he puzzles things out. While he eats he eats at a table; where he sleeps he sleeps in beds. If attended to in hospital, it's by a doctor, not vet. Since the ape and *Homo sapiens* may claim a common ancestry, he and his audience are kin. This is not so much a matter of the gene-pool as of attitude: his moods are moods we share. The well-meaning mischievous monkey, the child whom curiosity imperils but cannot kill, the creature from another world so much at home in the human one: George does not change or age.

Which is less than entirely true. For openers his name has been changed, and to begin with he played a supporting not a starring role. George started life as Fifi, one of nine monkeys who befriend a giraffe—called Rafi in France and Cecily in England. *Rafi et les Neuf Singes. Cecily G. and the Nine Monkeys.* The other members of the family were "Mother Pamplemoose and Baby Jinny, James who was good, Johnny who was brave, Arthur who was kind, David who was strong, and Punch and Judy, the twins." Of the ten characters in that first "adventure," Fifi/George is the one who survives; the giraffe and the other eight monkeys have been installed on the shelves of rare-book collectors or perhaps just gone back to the zoo.

In England, moreover, he was called Zozo. The reigning monarch at the time was George VI, and it would have been—to say the least—impolitic to use a king's name for a monkey, no matter how well-behaved. Further, in British slang of the early 1940s, a "curious" fellow was homosexual, and sex can't enter in. So the unchanging animal we read about and watch today had several incarnations *before* he was Curious George. Why he—and not, say, Whiteblack the Penguin or Pretzel the Dog (two more of his creators' creatures)—should have become so popular is a question well worth asking: Why should **X** succeed, **Y** muddle along, and **Z** fail?

His was in fact neither an instant nor an explosive success; it took years for Fifi-Zozo-George to take his place in the collective consciousness. Few figures in our culture are now more recognizable, but that was not always the case. Slowly, slyly, he caught on. Children responded rapidly; in the fullness of time, so did their own children and then their children's children. This business of name recognition—*Let me read you the book my parents read me*—is central to enduring popularity and why, say, *The Tale of Peter Rabbit* or *The Cat in the Hat* continues to claim our allegiance. George joins a special company—Mickey Mouse and Babar the Elephant among them—who move through generations yet stay young.

*

```
Dear M. REY. Thank you for writing Curious George
books. I like them and I read them. By Vanessa
```

*

Born in Hamburg, Germany, on 16 September 1898, Hans Augusto Reyersbach left to find work in Brazil. In 1924, in the harsh aftermath of World War I, there was little employment at home, and in any case the young ex-soldier embraced what Germans call a *wanderjahre*. It grew, though not entirely of his own choosing, into "wander-years." Skilled in languages and a gifted linguist—he knew Latin and Greek, as well as French and English, a smattering of Russian and, soon, Portuguese—Hans carried his sketchbook and pipe. He had been fond of animals always; always, he wanted to paint.

In his "first recognizable drawing," made when barely two years old, there were "Men on Horseback." By his own attestation, "Both men and horse had human faces." As he put it in an answer to a questionnaire ("The Life of H. A. Rey, told by himself in Chronological Order"): "1924: Matters having gone from bad to worse, I accepted a job offered me by relatives in their import firm in Brazil. I thus found myself composing commercial letters (which I was not allowed to adorn with illustrations) and selling bathtubs up and down the Amazon River. Obviously it was not the right road but it took me twelve years to find that out."

In 1935 Margarete Waldstein also traveled to South America and, on arrival in Rio de Janeiro, looked up her Hamburg acquaintance. He was eight years her senior and knew an older sister. Before the advent of the Third Reich and its all-leveling horror, the Waldsteins were prosperous people: five children, a house full of books. According to their story, Hans first met Margarete in her large family home when she slid down a banister; that antic disposition stayed with her all her life. Whether she "set her cap" for him or was simply looking for a *landsman* in a distant land we are unlikely to know.

In the mid 1930s, displacement was the new rule. This would no doubt have deepened their affinity: two strangers in a far-off place who shared a natal home. Both were painters—he self-taught and she with formal Bauhaus training in photography and art. It must have been romantic: alone together in a brave new world, remembering the long cold winters, the River Alster, and the ship-clogged Hamburg port. It must have been difficult also; what information they could glean from Germany was bad and growing worse. The courtship was a rapid one and, in August 1935, they wed.

Restless and ambitious, Margarete persuaded Hans to give up his work in import-export and join her in an advertising venture. As she stated in her own brief CV, "Went to Rio de Janeiro, Brazil. Started working with H. A. Rey who was to become my husband later. We wrote newspaper articles and advertisements, did posters, photography—anything that came our way." Her partner described it as a "Turning Point, 1935: A girl from my home town, disliking things in Nazi Germany, showed up under Rio's palm trees. Before three months had passed I was not only married to her but had said goodbye to commerce."

All accounts of the couple have them well-matched—he gentle, unassuming, and already balding, she red-haired and freckled and fierce. There are those who see the face he gave to Curious George—bright-eyed, smiling, snub-nosed, broad—as an image of his wife. If so, the portrait she sat for is in equal measure cartoon and homage; the face is portrayed with affection. One early business card (August 1935) is a drawing of a camera and paintbrush with a walking easel. The legend reads *Grüsse Von*

Hans Reyersbach und Frau Margarete, geb. Waldstein (Greetings from Hans Reyersbach and wife Margarete, born Waldstein.) For the convenience of clients, and as a way to forge a shared commercial identity, the couple soon renamed themselves H. A. and Margret Rey.

Intending to spend a brief honeymoon period in Paris, the Reys stayed for four years. As Brazilian citizens and with Brazilian passports, they took lodgings in the Terrass Hotel on the Rue Joseph de Maistre, Apartment 505. Montmartre proved congenial: she took photographs; he drew. As a form of self-expression but with commercial ambitions, they wrote and illustrated children's books. These were, at best, a marginal success. Not until they settled on a monkey did they settle down and in.

The special magic of Curious George was therefore conjured by a pair of artists who used their own experience to write of innocence. Hans Augusto Reyersbach and Margarete Waldstein—though few now know them by those names—are household figures today. From Hamburg, Germany, where they were born, to Cambridge, Massachusetts, where they died, is a long, eventful trip. These lines recount that journey and some stops along the way.

*

From Tommy Spang, Grade IV, an essay on "My Monkey":

```
When I was one year old I got a monkey. His name
was Curious George. I got him for my birthday
from my mother. I can never go to bed without
him! He makes a nice pillow for me. When he was
new he was brown and furry. He had a big fat
mouth. Now he is flat and holey. He lives on my
bed in the daytime and in my bed at night. He has
been on an airplane three times with me.
```

*

The travels would continue, as would their travails. When war was formally declared in September 1939, the Reys moved out of harm's way in Paris, and settled in southwest France. Mistakenly, after four months near the Pyrenees, they thought returning would be safe and went back to their apartment on the Rue Joseph de Maistre. By January 1940, working on *Whiteblack the Penguin* and *The Adventures of Fifi,* they had amassed a dossier of drawings and were in touch with publishers, Chatto and Windus in London and, in Paris, the Librarie Hachette and Gallimard. Briefly, they sojourned in Avranches, on the edge of Normandy and near Mont St. Michel. On 23 May 1940, they returned to Paris for a final time: a city under siege. It was declared an "open city," by which the authorities meant they would make no attempt at defense as the German army approached. By mid-June two million Parisians had fled south, and the Reys completed preparations—acquiring passports, visas, cards of identity, as much cash as they could withdraw from local banks—for escape. From adventurers self-exiled, they became true refugees.

The trains were full, or canceled. They owned no car. The roads were in any case clogged, impassable, and taxis nowhere to be found. For the price of a month's lodging at the Terrass—1,600 francs—Rey bought spare parts for two bicycles and, under the watchful eye of the owner in the *velo* store, assembled them. With no prior training as a mechanic, he must have been handy with tools: the tires, the handlebars, pedals, the seat, and gears all had to be properly fitted; it's the sort of ingenuity George would later on display. Prudentially as well, Rey bought four saddlebags. He was past forty, no longer young, and though there might have been a whiff of adventure in the planned evacuation, it must have been mostly a horror: no sense of when they'd be arrested or where assaulted, no foreknowledge of terrain.

The departure was cold and wet and slow; they slept in barns, depending on the kindness of French strangers, finally crossing the border into Spain. In their saddlebags the couple packed what bread and water they could carry, and also the books they were working on and could not bear to jettison. Once, as they later recalled it, they were stopped by a suspicious border official who, demanding papers, leafed through the series of drawings and decided that the two of them could not be enemy agents or likely to cause harm.

For a publicity brochure for Houghton Mifflin, their American publishers, they later wrote:

In June 1940, on a rainy morning before dawn, a few hours before the Nazis entered, we left Paris on bicycles, with nothing but warm coats and our manuscripts [*Curious George* among them] tied to the baggage racks, and started pedaling south. We finally made it to Lisbon, by train, having sold our bicycles to custom officials at the French-Spanish border. After a brief interlude in Rio de Janeiro, our migrations came to an end one clear, crisp October morning in 1940, when we saw the Statue of Liberty rise above the harbor of New York and landed in the U.S.A.

*

Dear Mr. Rey.
I have your four books about C. G. I mean Curious George and Ceciely G. and the nine monkeys, I don't mean Charles Gibbs. I wrote you once before when I was in fourth grade. Now I am in fifth grade. I am going to Daniel Webster School. I liked the book you wrote, so will you pleas send me a of all the book you wrote, and if you know any books you'er going to write. Thank you for your photo you sent me when you wrote me beofer. Pleas send your first and second name.
Sincerely yours, Charles A. Gibbs 3rd.
[Spelling errors retained.]

*

The first of the books with Rey's name on the spine (copyright, 1941) begins: "This is George. He lived in Africa. He was a good little monkey / and always very curious." The "good" here is important. Although he causes and routinely gets into trouble, George *means* well. He's impish, yes, but not an imp of the perverse. His adventures and wild escapades prove finally harmless, his curiosity nonlethal; the endings are happy ones, always, and each of the problems gets solved. In every one of the volumes, a generous gesture takes stage center: decency abounds. A certain kind of children's tale—think of the Brothers Grimm, or Hans Christian Andersen—is darker, menace-filled. Others in the German tradition—Till Eulenspiegel, *Struwwelpeter* (wild-haired Peter), Max and Moritz—deal with troublemakers whose virtue is not unalloyed. But George "was a good little monkey" and he stays that way.

Another signal attribute is his great agility. *Because* of his simian competence—his ability to leap, scale heights, catch objects on the fly—he can solve problems mere humans cannot: he climbs a tall tree to rescue a bear, a kite gets retrieved from a branch. George can wriggle through apertures where we'd get stuck, can jump from roof to roof. And since his role in the family of man is that of wordless baby, it's doubly satisfying to his audience that he should also prove skilled. These are tales where, though things go awry, peace reigns. Pandora's box gets closed. In a world so often threat-filled, it matters to a child that such stories end in dreamless sleep; his adventures conclude in domesticity, and always in the end our hero is welcomed back. He creates disorder, then order; out of chaos, he retrieves calm.

The narrative starts with displacement; George has to cross the sea. Born in Africa, he cannot stay. He's captured and transported and, on the ship, escapes; he survives near-death by drowning when watchful sailors haul him back aboard their ship. The despot with a yellow hat who caught and brought him "home" turns out to be a kindly man who befriends the little monkey and rescues him from peril. That Hans Augusto Reyersbach and Margarete Waldstein, his Jewish co-creators, had a narrow escape from the Nazis, fleeing across the ocean in 1940, is surely no coincidence. That they too reached safe haven and changed their names—becoming H. A. and Margret Rey—is also not an accident. Theirs was a life of exile and, thereafter, self-invention; as German Jewish refugees they left their own dark continent and began anew.

After the first volume in the series, six more "original" texts were published between 1947 and 1966. They are, in order, *Curious George Takes a Job, Curious George Rides a Bike, Curious George Gets a Medal, Curious George Flies a Kite, Curious George Learns the Alphabet,* and *Curious George Goes to the Hospital.* Without over-large a critical leap, it's possible to argue that each of these titles has personal resonance; the Reys escaped from Paris on a pair of homemade bicycles; their "job" had to do with the alphabet, and it was one for which they earned medals. H. A. Rey studied wind-power and taught astronomy if not the construction of kites; he died, beloved of the nursing staff, in a Boston hospital.

That marriage is a partnership has become a truism; that partners should collaborate so closely in creative work is rare. The venture was collaborative, always; always, they made books together. He did the drawings and she told the stories, though it's difficult to parse with total certainty who did what. Often, both did both. The Reys' careers were long, their interests various, but curiosity is constant and embodied in their title character.

Who lives on.

*

```
Dear H. A. Rey:
I hope you write some more stories about George.
I like all of your stories about him. I wish I
could see you in real life. But I guess it does
not matter. Your friend, Eric
```

*

At present there are seventy-five million copies of books about our affable scamp, in nearly twenty languages, and George survives his original makers. Indeed, the series includes more titles composed and published *after* the Reys (H. A. Rey died in 1977, Margret in 1996) than was the case during their lifetimes. In Cambridge, Massachusetts, at a landmark location in Harvard Square, a store stands wholly devoted to Curious George. It sells more than books. The backpacks and stuffed animals and cups and caps and sweatshirts and toys, the boxed sets of CDs and DVDs have become an industry, a horn of plenty with the little monkey bestride it like a colossus, smiling. Or, to shift the metaphor, the sun never sets upon the empire of George; through publishing ventures and daily television programs, theatricals, theme-park rides, mass-market and specialized merchandise, he has enlarged his domain.

In their most optimistic imaginings, the Reys could not have dreamed of such a profitable afterlife. Just past the seventy-fifth anniversary of the first publication in English of *Curious George,* his youthful antics persist. Margret was, among other things, a canny businesswoman, and she negotiated hard and well. The archive is chock-a-block full of dealings with publishers and production companies and lawsuits: no detail too small to attend to, no royalty foregone. But these commercial transactions seem somehow in the service of unfettered innocence; the world traversed by our inquisitive monkey is one without class standing or economic strata. He's neither—to pick just two examples—Eloise at the Plaza nor little Orphan Annie; he moves with border-crossing ease from poverty to luxury, abundance to constraint. Childless, the couple now speaks to children everywhere. Impoverished, they grew rich.

What follows is an alphabetical list of licensees for *Curious George,* as of 22 September 1997. More have been issued since. These are only the first few contractual agreements, having to do with Book Stores, Stationery Stores, and Gift Store Distributions; the list's entries should be sufficient, however, to display the little monkey's large commercial range:

AMERICAN GREETINGS	Christmas ornaments, paper gift bags, wrapping paper; stickers, assorted Valentine cards . . .
AMERICAN SPECIALTY	Gift tins with snacks, sweets
ANTIOCH	Book plates, book marks, journals, locked diaries
ARTISTIC GREETINGS	Personalized note paper, note pads, etc.
BLUE Q	Magnets
CLASSICO SAN FRANCISCO	Postcards
CREATIVE EXPRESSIONS	Party goods, invitations, treat sacks, etc.
DANFORTH PEWTER	Pewter keychain, ornaments, picture frames
DAYDREAM/LANDMARK	Calendars, posters
DOVER PUBLICATIONS	Paper doll book
EVERY PICTURE TELLS A STORY	Limited edition prints
GLITTERWRAP	Wrapping paper, gift bags, enclosures
GRAPHIQUE DE FRANCE	Posters, prints, note cards, wall calendars, gift cards, postcards, gift T-shirts
GTA/PRINTWICK PAPERS	Magnets, notepads, pins
INKADINKADO	Rubber stamps and stamp sets

There are licensing arrangements with Specialty Toy Stores (Alma Designs, ALPI, Applause, Basic Fun, Curiosity Kits, Disguise, etc.) and Apparel and Accessories (Accessory Network, ACI, Adorable Lingerie, American Marketing, American Needle, Bag Bazaar, etc.), with Domestics, Room Décor and House-wares (Belinda Barton, Jay Franco, Pure Country, Santa Barbara, Selandei/Zak Designs, etc.) and a whole raft of Entertainment Media and Educational Markets. By contract, the estate licenses and profits from cloth play activity sets, squeeze toy figurines, key chains, Halloween costumes, cube and boxed puzzles, stuffed dolls of all types, puzzles, board games and table games, peel-and-press stickers, playsets, bags, footwear, hats, mittens, scarves, children's baseball hats, silk and polyester ties, umbrellas, cos-metic bags, watches, clocks, infant and toddler apparel sets and separates.

The list goes on: seek a collectible china cookie jar, a chil-dren's miniature Afghan blanket, infant bedding, a plush back-pack, Fruit of the Loom underwear and socks, a melamine dining set or soft-sided lunch kit, a beanbag or hand puppet in Sweden, and Curious George is your man.

*

```
Dear Mr. H. A. Rey: Why do they call you that?
And what did your Mummy call you, H. or A.?  By
Andy.
```

*

My parents too were refugees from Hitler's Germany. They met again and married in London, then settled—in the late 1940s, with two young sons—in a suburb of New York. Visitors would share their stories: whose relatives were lost or had survived, who prospered or were failing, and who needed help.

One such couple, I remember, had a romantic history; they had escaped from Paris only a few hours before Nazis seized the city. The man—like my father—had been born in Hamburg, and he was good at drawing and had a childlike eye. According to

my parents (though I of course could not address them so infor-
mally) his name was Hans, hers Margarete, and they had written
books about a penguin and giraffe and dachshund and then a
monkey called Curious George.

By the time they came to see us, the Reys were famous and
well-off. I remember my mother served more than usually abun-
dant pastries, and that she used the good china and told me to
wear a clean shirt.

Mr. Rey was plump, in a brown suit, and he wore glasses and
a comb-over and was round-faced and kind. He had a manner
with children both easy and unforced. He knew about the stars
and, in 1952, would publish a book about them; on a previous
visit he had taken me into the garden and shown me constellations in a way that made me *see*. We were sitting in the living
room, and he stood off to one side. Suddenly, I heard, "Nicky,
help! It's Curious George and I'm stuck in the fireplace and can't
move. Come help me, won't you please?"

I looked around. Mrs. Rey, unconcerned, drank her tea. But
Mr. Rey, upright by the piano, had a strained expression on his
face; his Adam's apple bobbed up and down, and his lips twitched
soundlessly.

"Tommy!"—now it was my older brother's turn to be
addressed—"It's the Man with the Yellow Hat, and I'm looking
for Curious George and can't find him anywhere. Where do you
think he might be?"

This went on for some time. Turn by turn we were cajoled
by creatures from a story book, and even then I knew enough to
know I was supposed to act surprised. We boys jumped up and
looked in the fireplace chimney; we tried to pretend the man
in our living room—I had watched Edgar Bergen and Char-
ley McCarthy and knew about ventriloquists—was *not* playing
Curious George. He was very bad at it. He squeaked and per-
spired and moved his mouth, and only when he said goodbye
and wiped his face and shrugged himself into his overcoat did
he seem an adult again. I remember thinking, as I watched them
drive away in their fine clothes and gleaming car, well, a per-

son can get rich by pretending to be someone else and then by throwing his voice.

"Voice." I have been trying to throw it all my writing life. Ventriloquists are few and far between, and very few are good at it, and authors don't routinely work in distant vocal registers. Yet in some central way I date my love of the profession to the sight and sound of H. A. Rey being foolish in our living room—a Pied Piper in a tailored suit who, together with his artist-wife, constructed an enchantment for the young. Each time I light a fire now I think of that invented creature hidden in the chimney and ready to leap to the page.

*

```
Dear H. A. Rey
How are you feeling? Are writing more books?
Please send me some of your picture and some
book covers. I am in third grade. I have a nice
teacher. Her name is Mrs. Spilko. My name is
Delores. I like to read your books about Curi-
ous George.
Your friend Delores Shelton
```

*

Rey answered such letters often—and often appended a sketch. Most of those who wrote him did so in a childish hand, using large block letters and writing on ruled sheets; some few lines of praise were transcribed by parents or teachers. Often, whole classes sent letters for forwarding to the offices of Houghton Mifflin, and packets of fan-mail arrived. There were frequent questions. One librarian, a Carolyn McRory in Florence, Alabama, wondered (on 9 November 1973) why George has no tail.

Rey's answer is worth reprinting: "Well—George never had a tail, nor, for that matter, do chimpanzees, orangutans, gorillas, gibbons, samangos, cape monkeys. George himself doesn't belong to any of those species—he is a creature of my imagination, the size of a small chimp and the color, more or less, of an orangutan. Artistic license."

And even when there's an objection lodged, as in a highly censorious letter from a woman in Topeka, Kansas, who frowns upon the trouble that curiosity engenders and says his books encourage it (11 November 1975), he answers, "Yet one has to keep one's sense of humor, don't you agree? Especially in times like these, and I wish you and your four-year old son, as well as his grandmother (who certainly meant well when she gave him the book), a very happy 1976."

*

Every so often George dons a costume—a window-washer's cap and belt, a parachutist's regalia—but most of the time he stays naked, clothed in his brown fur. His age is uncertain yet more or less constant; he will not sport a beard. The first time we see him is how he continues to look; like his protector, the "Man with the Yellow Hat," he will neither thicken nor stoop. The creature who works on a puzzle at the end of the Reys' last volume has the shape and semblance of the monkey who eats a banana on the first page of the first. In the category to which his story belongs— illustrated children's literature—a protagonist does not submit to alteration or even shifts of emphasis; he must be recognizable, a figure we can point to: *Look, Mommy, it's Curious George!*

The central mystery here is one that need not be explained: how a man and a monkey converse. It's a one-way conversation, but it works. We take for granted, simply, that the Man with the Yellow Hat says things to George that George comprehends, and to which he can respond. Aloud, the animal says nothing— never will, in any of the books—but communication between the two is nonetheless oral; what the man proposes is something his new companion smilingly agrees to, then tries—and often fails— to obey. (The exception to this rule comes in *Cecily G. and the Nine Monkeys,* in which Fifi also speaks. By the time he's a solo performer, however, George stays mute.) The human need not learn sign language or acquire the skill-set of nonverbal discourse; he speaks as might a parent to an infant or young child. And the monkey understands. Expressive in action, he need not use words; the back-and-forth between the pair feels as natural as chatter between close friends or members of a family. That they don't share a species is beside the story's point.

This logic-defying arrangement is established from the start, a ground-rule of the game, and the reader never questions its validity. To do so would be to engage in animal behavior studies or to examine the extent of a monkey's adaptive capacity when brought in from the jungle. George reacts to the call of the tame, not wild; it takes a while to notice he can't speak. These are issues for zoologists and behavioral psychologists, perhaps, but not for the readers of *Curious George*. Throughout, his actions are human, not simian, and this holds true all along.

*

Dear Mr. H. A. Rey: What did you do to become that good of a writer? What made you want to write Curious George books? Did you ever have a monkey? I like the nice pictures. Your pal, John Howard

*

Time, now, to look more carefully at the seven books. They are parts of a collective whole, and like all components of a series have some overlap. But each of *The Adventures of Curious George* is self-sufficient and each merits close attention.

(1) *Curious George,* 1941

The language here is simple. Later, the juxtaposition of text to image will grow more intricate, but in this first installment the left-hand page consists of narrative and the right-hand page a picture. What we're told about on the left-hand side we see illustrated on the right. Almost all the words are monosyllabic or disyllabic; the word "curious," with its trisyllabic pronunciation, stands out. A very few other "big" or three-syllable words festoon the pages: "overboard," "telephoned," "firemen," "department," "quietly," and "quieted." In the book's fifty pages there are two words with four syllables—"fascinated" and "altogether"—but the vast majority of verbiage is pitched to the young ear.

Hans Reyersbach was something of a linguist. As he wrote by way of self-assessment, "Besides being fluent in English, German, French and Portuguese, I have a working knowledge of Latin, Classical Greek, Spanish, Italian, Dutch, and fundamentals of Russian and Rumanian." If not a polymath, he was at ease with polysyllabic utterance—so the "Basic English" discourse here is one of conscious choice. It helped, perhaps, that he and his wife composed the text in a language not their natal one; the simplicity of diction feels both unforced and apt. It's not as if they bite their tongues in order to avoid such terms as "polysyllabic utterance"; the story is meant for a young audience—roughly three to seven years old. And those words that might require explanation—"fascinated, altogether"—are easy to define.

We see George eating a banana on page 1; by page 26 he's eating soup with a spoon, seated at a table with a carafe of water and bottle of wine; afterwards, in a green plush chair, he smokes a pipe, then dons a pair of pajamas and snuggles into bed. Technically, what we have here is anthropomorphism: the ascription of human characteristics to things not human. The monkey is a boy-child, though he may not look like one. It's also true, of course, that the boy-child is a monkey, and many of his antics will be monkeyshines. And here is where the secondary meaning of *curious—strange—*pertains; it's strange to see an animal behaving with such nonchalance in the human context. Though I doubt the Reys considered this, they forged "the missing link."

The question of "mastery" must be addressed. George is conscripted into civilization, not a volunteer. The man with "a large yellow straw hat" begins the action with entrapment; he places his headgear on the ground, "and, of course, George was curious." So he tries on the hat and cannot remove it and gets caught. It had not been his plan or desire to leave Africa; volition here is entirely the captor's. "I would like to take him home with me," the man decides. Not until they reach the ship does he dispense with his gun.

We should not make over-much of this. Few stories are better humored or less menace-and-grief filled; to describe this as a form of slavery or even a simple abduction is to miss the point. Those critics who construe the tale as a parable of empire and servitude are, in my opinion, wrong. When rowed "across the water to a big ship . . . George was sad, but he was still a little curious." The illustration has him smiling, staring at fish, and the Man with the Yellow Hat throws a protective arm around his shoulder; his mouth, too, has turned up. The sailor who rows them to their waiting vessel sports a gap-toothed grin. When George dives overboard, escaping the ship that takes him far from home, it's because he wants to fly as sea gulls do, and "he HAD to try." This is no captive's desperate bid for freedom but an excited creature's ill-judged escapade. The crew-members throwing a life belt cry, "Man [not monkey] overboard!" Equating him with any other passenger, they rush to set things right.

And when, after a long journey, the steamship attains the American shore, it's George who happily strides down the gangplank in front, carrying his passport and a bag. Behind him steps the Man with the Yellow Hat, likewise with a suitcase and papers, though again with his rifle strapped to his back. Third in line follows a porter with their additional luggage. The sailors wave a cheerful goodbye, the dockhands stare up at them smilingly, and the official saluting on shore is delighted, clearly, to make these passengers welcome. The party has arrived.

How innocent it all seems now; how easy their arrival! Imagine, for an instant, what would happen on the New York docks if a man with a gun and a monkey tried to disembark today. All difficulties of transport and immigration are resolved by the gesture of turning a page; *Hey presto,* we've come home! And, once installed, the easy domesticity of this "odd couple" sets the stage for adventures abroad. The trouble George gets into in this first installment—a fire alarm, a cluster of helium-filled balloons that carry him away—is trouble caused by ignorance that has its root in innocence: How does a telephone work? Why should balloons lift the monkey who holds their strings aloft?

The first book has three such instances. George falls overboard; he sets off a false fire alarm and goes to jail; he rises perilously high above the city while holding a bunch of balloons. Each of these three mishaps is occasioned by enthusiasm, an excess of zeal, and this will always prove true. The moral or instruction is *Be careful*: Don't rush over-fast into things. And each suggests a learning curve: don't try to fly, don't use machinery you haven't learned the purpose of, don't let your reach exceed your grasp. It's easy enough to translate all this into a didactic text, but the lessons of *Curious George* are rarely so explicit; these stories have no final or summary assertion. Instead we have an image of George falling into the sea, an image of firemen chasing through streets, an image of jail and his escape along telephone wires, an image of him soaring high. We *picture* his trouble; we *watch* him at risk; we *see* how things go wrong. And then we watch them set right.

Soon we'll come to take for granted that such escapades end well. False fire alarms and jail cells and near-death by drowning or falling from heights all are perilous, but George survives his mishaps handily. Equilibrium at adventure's end gets restored, and it's a very different thing from, say, the lament of Epaminondas's mother: *You ain't got the sense you was born with!* Our hero learns fast; he won't make the same mistake twice (which is one of the reasons the books are wide-ranging; each predicament is new). And though we cannot imagine precisely what fix he'll find himself in, we know it can be fixed.

For children, there's real pleasure in predictability. As soon as the man with the large yellow hat—that perfect parental figure, who never loses his temper—picks up the phone to make a call, we guess the watchful monkey will tackle the instrument too. In this regard, and to the degree that children's books are a kind of instruction manual, the seven volumes of the adventures of *Curious George* comprise an education. What's constant is his curiosity; what changes is the trouble he gets into, and it is never the same. He doesn't follow, to start with, the details of adult transaction, but misunderstanding will be remedied and lost balloons get paid for; he'll play by society's rules.

And this is part of the dramatic arc of each installment: the monkey gets into and gets out of trouble, always emerging the wiser; always he's forgiven for the mess he made and the fuss he caused. The books' titular topics—*get a job, ride a bicycle, go to the hospital,* and so forth—are instructive, and more and more consciously so. By the end of the series, for instance, the Reys were trying to prepare their audience for hospital stays by making such strangeness familiar. And *Curious George Learns the Alphabet* is a primer for young readership; the illustrations move from **A** to **Z** until even the analphabetic monkey starts to write, substituting *ten* bags of doughnuts for the requested *one.* In some sense, therefore, what George learns in each installment is what children must learn too; by making his incautious way through the complicated adult world, he lets his readers follow where he leads.

Another part of the drama has to do with coincidence, or corner-cutting. It's improbable, in *Curious George,* that the first time he attempts to dial he calls the Fire Department—or no more probable than that a monkey sitting at a typewriter could bang out Hamlet's soliloquy: *To be or not to be.* It's improbable, as well, that a man would be selling balloons just outside a prison wall (not to mention that a little girl would be buying a balloon for her little brother.) The city is unnamed and, to a degree, generic; it resembles a stripped-down New York. Which makes it improbable, finally, that the Man with the Yellow Hat would be driving his blue car and caught in the very traffic jam his flyaway monkey occasions.

These narrative shortcuts belong to the genre, but they suggest a well-made world where things fall into place. Few problems take much longer than a turned page to resolve. The final image of the first installment has George sitting happily in the crook of a tree in a "ZOO! What a nice place for George to live!" All around him are animals—elephants, giraffes, flamingos, lions, polar bears—playing with balloons. It's surely the cluster just purchased and, on arrival, distributed; the moral here is "Share!"

(2) *Curious George Takes a Job*, 1947

The first illustration of the second volume shows George in a cage, swinging on a trapeze. The cage has a blue chair, a green ball, and yellow cutlery on a blue table; the sign affixed to his enclosure reads: "**Curious George. Monkey (Africa)**." What follows is an intricate narrative filled with new adventures; he sets out to see the world. The language is roughly akin to that of volume one—monosyllabic, disyllabic, with a few larger words such as "discovered," "elephant," and "forever"—but now the left-hand/right-hand alignment of story line and picture has been rendered more complex. Sometimes the language is printed above an illustration, sometimes beneath, sometimes between two pictures on a page. What's notably more complicated is the motivation: George yearns to leave confinement and live with his friend, the Man with the Yellow Hat, whose address he does not yet know.

Therefore he escapes from the zoo. First, he hides in the hay of the elephant cage, then runs out and hops on a bus. Atop the bus, he stares with interest at his new surroundings—this cityscape so different from the world he left behind. Once in the center of town, and feeling very hungry, he goes into a restaurant and eats "yards and yards" of what the cook has been preparing: a huge pot of spaghetti. Affable, the cook does not scold but makes him wash dishes and clean up the mess, praising his "four hands"—George uses both feet also—and then commending him to a friend who "could use a handy little fellow like you to wash windows." (Again, and at the risk of repetition, it's notable that the cook doesn't shout, *There's a monkey in my kitchen.* Instead, and like all the other adults in the story, he deals with the animal on human terms, conversing with him as naturally as did the Man with the Yellow Hat.) Soon, the elevator operator in a skyscraper hires George, first warning him not to be curious or stare through the windows he's washing—a warning we know the monkey will be unable to heed.

A little boy who doesn't eat his spinach and a man asleep both fail to engage his attention, though he wishes that the sleeping man were his absent friend. The third window (always, in such fables, it's the third) does give him pause. "Two painters were working inside." Beguiled by the prospect of bright pots of color and blank white walls, George takes advantage of the painters' lunch break and, picking up a paintbrush, recreates the jungle he called home.

He's very good at it; his artistry mimics the Reys'. His illustrations look just like other pictures in the book. Enthusiastic, George transforms draped furniture into a zebra, a leopard, a giraffe; he paints palm trees and grass and birds. He's working on the portrait of a little monkey ("busy painting himself on one of the trees!") when the hired painters return. Outraged at the mess he's made of their pristine labor, the workers give chase—as does the woman who owns the apartment, the elevator man, and a whole host of others. Fleet-footed George escapes them and jumps from the bottom of the fire escape, but fails to understand the pavement is not made of grass. For the first time we see him injured, and with his feelings hurt. From the monkey's visage, teardrops fall.

Next we see him in an ambulance and then a hospital, since he has broken his leg. After some time, it heals. But his misadventures continue; he's tempted by a bottle of ether and, sniffing it, loses his balance again. Meanwhile, the Man with the Yellow Hat has read the newspapers about "A Monkey Hurt in Fall" and arrives to collect him; a kind doctor and a nurse have taken good care of their patient and wave George on his way. Here it's worth noting that the sidewalk newsstand blazons the story; various editions read "Monkey Goes to Hospital," "Monkey Paints Room," "Monkey Taken To Hospital With Broken Leg." That George's escapade would dominate the papers is of course unlikely, but we are reminded of the animal nature of our hero. Worth noting, too: the whole city is transfixed. George is a "headliner" and soon will be a movie star; if large crowds read about and watch him, then his young audience can read the headlines too . . .

As with the first installment, there's a chase. In *Curious George* the monkey fails to outdistance his pursuers (firemen) because he gets tangled in a telephone cord; in *Curious George Takes a Job,* he's undone by concrete. As a plot device, this is necessary: if George were to escape and not be caught, there would be no punishment and therefore no subsequent reward. After the first chase, he goes to jail, after the second, to a hospital, and in both cases additional trouble ensues. We move from escapade to escapade and from trial to trial.

The next stop on his journey is a movie studio; the Man with the Yellow Hat has decided to make a film about his charge, and the president of the studio has George sign a contract. (Again, as with the customs officials in the first book, the transition here is seamless; no sooner do they wish to make a movie than the deal is done. Again, reality gets tailored so as to make things simple; the movie mogul welcomes the pair, with no questions asked.) The monkey leans forward eagerly to sign; he's sitting on the lap of the yellow-garbed man, who is hatless; as a celebratory gesture—there are five phones on the president's desk!—the man foregoes his pipe and puffs on a cigar. The movie set is a fabricated jungle. George plays in it happily; we've moved, perhaps, to Hollywood—and the show goes on.

These illustrations are intricate; they showcase Rey's painterly gifts. The rendition of a skyscraper, the room George paints—evoking the jungle—the movie set where he descends from a tree to pick up the yellow hat, as he had done in the first installment: all these are depicted with real flair. The colors are bright, the outlines clear, the characters and caricatures incisive. On the page where George sniffs ether there are six separate illustrations, from the first where he sees the blue bottle to the fifth where he sees "rings and stars" and the last where "everything went dark." Five of the book's illustrations—the zoo, the city, the three-page sequence in the apartment—are double-leafed and emphasize horizontal action with, in effect, a spreadsheet. The majority of drawings occupy a single page, or a portion of a page; the palette-range is broad. Mostly we're dealing with primary colors, but George is brown, the man in the elevator wears a green coat and cap, the subway is black, the telephone booth salmon pink. No small part of the pleasure of *reading* these adventures is the pleasure of *seeing* them also; the pictures are vivid throughout.

By now our narrative terms have been established. The book begins with "This is George . . ." and the first page contains the phrase "always very curious." It ends with the same assertion; "This is George / He lived in the jungle / He was a good little monkey—he had only one fault: he was too curious." George has become a movie star (a prescient prediction by the Reys) and attends a gala opening of a film called *Curious George*. The last image of the second book shows a movie theater with George and the Man with the Yellow Hat—who has removed his sombrero out of courtesy to those seated behind—and a packed house. The picture on the screen shows a little monkey at the base of a palm tree fabricated on the set but evoking Africa; he's staring at the yellow hat within which he'll be trapped.

This is all very circular, very modern, and self-referential; we end where we began. (The same holds true for George's painterly efforts in the apartment and for the newspaper headlines; they reinforce by repetition what we've seen before.) One of the rewards of children's literature is the predictable phrase and recurrent refrain; George and curiosity have become ineluctably linked. It's his defining characteristic; it will carry him through each installment and, later, every TV show . . .

(3) *Curious George Rides a Bike,* 1952

All his life, Hans Reyersbach loved zoos. He frequented them often and always kept a pet or two; his other books star penguins, dachshunds, a giraffe. Again, from "The Life of H. A. Rey, told by himself . . ." "I lived near the [Hagenbeck] Zoo and soon was more familiar with elephants and kangaroos than with cows or sheep. I am still fond of animals and often go to the Zoo. I sometimes dream of having a small Zoo of my own, somewhere in the countryside." The Man with the Yellow Hat informs George, in Book One, that he will live in just such a supervised enclosure. That seems appropriate enough: the big-game hunter brings his captured trophy home. And Book Two begins: "This is George. He lived in the Zoo." (Every one of the volumes begins with the same three-word introduction: "This is George." Consistency counts.) By Book Three, however—*Curious George Rides a Bike*—the second sentence reads: "He lived with his friend, the man with the yellow hat."

So by the third installment it's clear that George has larger fish to fry. I mean by this that, as the action of the second book suggests, the zoo is a confinement from which the monkey must escape. In the third book—although it importantly features other animals—he's living with his "friend." This may have been a decision the Reys took when they decided to make "the adventures" a series; there would have been a finite space for George to occupy if he remained in a zoo. Or perhaps the authors understood from the beginning that the special charm of their project had to do with border-crossing. In any case, the domain enlarges, and the society depicted here is the urban world. More and more, the humanizing process—anthropomorphism—takes over; once he departs the zoo, he's less and less related by species to the company he keeps. As he becomes a member of a cohort, the family the monkey claims is the family of man.

At the start of this third text, we read that time has passed. George, however, looks the same. The Man with the Yellow Hat (though he's not wearing headgear at the breakfast table) says, "Today we are going to celebrate because just three years ago this day I brought you home with me from the jungle." This transpires on page 2; the two are eating cereal and drinking coffee; there's a banana on the table and, above it, the by-now-familiar picture of George at the base of a palm tree entranced by the abandoned-seeming hat. They will celebrate that evening—"I'll take you to the animal show"—but first there's a surprise. The man (now outside and again wearing his headgear) uncrates a blue bicycle as a gift. Then the man departs for work—we never know what occupation, precisely, he pursues in the professional world—and, waving, says: "Be careful with your new bike and keep close to the house while I am gone."

By now, of course, the reader knows that George will—out of enthusiasm, not malice—disobey. And trouble will ensue. For a page or two all's well; George practices his bike-riding skills—riding without the use of hands, riding backwards or on only one wheel—then joins up with a newsboy in the street. He promises to help deliver papers but gets distracted by a river at road's end. (The landscape here has been transformed from cityscape to that of a small town or village. We have single-family dwellings and grass-lined suburban streets. A baker wheels his wares down the sidewalk; a postman smiles at children; there are dogs on leashes and people in doorways, a homeowner raking his lawn.)

Instead of turning back and distributing his newspapers on the far side of the avenue, George continues down the riverbank; he wants to build a paper boat and, using his stack of undelivered papers, folds a flotilla of boats. There's a page with nine separate illustrations that provides a lesson in origami, transforming the "Morning Star" to a serviceable vessel—and soon enough, George empties his bag and watches his creations float downstream. Entranced by folded ships and ducks, he fails to watch where he is riding and collides with a rock and falls off. "Luckily, George was not hurt, but the front wheel of the bicycle was all out of shape and the tire was blown out."

He tries to ride the bicycle; it will not work. He tries to carry it; it weighs too much. He regrets his disobedience and sits and cries and then remembers he can ride the bike on its rear wheel like "a cowboy on a wild bronco." This he does. Smiling once more, and traveling some further distance down the road he encounters a tractor-trailer with what "looked like a Zoo on wheels." Two men jump out to greet him; the director of the traveling circus is impressed by George's acrobatics and invites him to become a member of the troupe. The handyman, Bob, repairs the bike. Once on the carnival grounds (a double-sheet with mobile cages holding a seal, a hippopotamus, an elephant, leopard, ostrich, giraffe, and kangaroo), George is invited to "get acquainted with all the animals" but to make certain not to feed them, especially the ostrich. Who will eat anything on offer and get sick . . .

This amounts to an open invitation; we know before the page is turned that George will approach the ostrich with whatever he has to hand. He does not do so malevolently but out of curiosity, providing a bugle to see if the ostrich can play. Trying to swallow it, the ostrich gets the bugle stuck in his throat; he turns blue in the face. On the next page men rescue him, extracting the instrument; the director complains about George's misbehavior and says he's irresponsible and therefore can't join the show.

Punishment ensues. What follows is a new note—in terms of both the animal's reaction and his emotional register: "George had to sit on a bench all by himself and nobody even looked at him. He was terribly sorry for what he had done but now it was too late. He had spoiled everything." This scene was presaged by his tears after the accident on his bike; the Reys describe a growing if still childlike awareness of responsibility. Whereas the Man with the Yellow Hat is always all-forgiving, that's less true of other adults. Encountering disapproval, George must grow self-aware.

Soon enough, redemption follows. The ostrich gobbles at a string on the bear cage, releasing a baby bear who runs off to a high tree near the camp. George blows his bugle to alert show personnel and rides after the animal on his bike; here the chase is one he institutes, and he is the pursuer, not the pursued. Next he climbs the tree where the bear hangs at risk and puts him in the yellow bag that once held newspapers. The illustration of the rescue is a happy one: George hangs upside down from a branch, holding on with his curled feet; he lowers the bear in the yellow sack to three men below. All we see of the bystanders are upraised sleeves, but it's clear from their six waiting hands the baby bear will be brought safely to ground level. In his "Morning Star" sack, the bear smiles; so does the monkey at page-top. There's a caterpillar on a leaf, no doubt glad to watch this spectacle: "Everybody cheered."

So George is after all invited to perform in the animal show which his friend had promised, that morning, they would see. He rides his bike, balancing on the rear wheel; he wears a green coat and a cap and blows the yellow bugle. Behind him comes the ostrich, with the baby bear riding comfortably on the animal's back; in the audience, applauding, sit the newsboy and the Man with the Yellow Hat. There's a glad reunion; the newsboy gets his bag again, the townspeople forgive George for having lost their newspapers, and he and his friend embrace.

The next image is a double sheet, with a signpost on the left-hand page shaped like a pointing finger, reading **HOME!** And on the right-hand page the man and monkey drive their blue convertible. On the backseat sits the bicycle; in the bottom right-hand corner a small George, wearing pajamas and carrying his bugle, prepares to go to bed. The final illustration has him safely in his bed once more, with the bugle and the bicycle beside him on the floor. The legend reads *Good Night!*

In his three years "in captivity," George has matured a little. He understands what it means to be punished; his impulse to rescue the baby bear seems both protective and responsible. He's a glad participant in the traveling menagerie, but not a member thereof. The first book is a travel-tale, the second a story of adaptation. This third installment is circular, concluding where it began. What was lost is found.

(4) *Curious George Gets a Medal,* 1957

I have been treating the separate books as though they were part of a sequence—which to some degree they are. The seventieth anniversary edition of *The Adventures of Curious George* (2011) prints all seven original installments seriatim, and there's a way in which this makes good sense—as though the individual chapters comprise a single whole. Too, it's probably the case that any devotee of our inquisitive monkey will have read and owned more than one—perhaps all seven—of his adventures. As I wrote to begin with: "George does not change or age."

But it's also the case that all of these installments are intended to be self-sufficient, and each of them no doubt attracted a new audience. The five-year-old who loved *Curious George* would have grown beyond him by the time *Curious George Gets a Medal* appeared. The infant too young for the former would have turned sixteen by the time the latter appeared. The Reys were busy and productive, but they had other interests; there's a quarter of a century between the first (1941) and the final (1966) of the seven books. This is scarcely the rate of production that describes most serial publications, or the appearance of sequels to the "original" set. After 1966 (though Margret would not die for three more decades) they stopped. It's almost as though they felt compelled to return only every few years to the well—that wellspring of profit and pleasure which never did run dry. And just as each installment starts with the phrase, "This is George," each of the adventures reaches closure; in the fourth iteration, we begin again.

This fourth book, published in 1957, is much more "modern" than its predecessors. We see television sets and space suits and rocket-launching stations, radar and parachutes. After the by-now-predictable complications—of which more later—the

experiment concludes in triumph; George becomes "the first living being to come back to earth from a space flight." The action
reflects what had been happening in space exploration programs—to start with in the United States, then in France and
the Soviet Union. It was not a happy story for those monkeys
sent aloft.

In the first such journey, a rhesus monkey, Albert, rode on
a V2 rocket for nearly forty miles; he died of suffocation on a
flight on 11 June 1948. Albert II, a year later (14 June 1949) survived his flight but died on impact after his parachute failed;
Albert III died on 16 September 1949, in an explosion at thirty-
five thousand feet. On the last "monkey-manned" V2 flight, on
8 December of that year, Albert IV died on impact when his
parachute, too, failed. The photographs of monkeys and chimpanzees trussed up for their journey look very much like George
in his space suit, and the illustration of the launchpad looks
(though reduced and simplified) like the actual thing.

Next, monkeys flew on Aerobee rockets. A monkey died
due to parachute failure on 18 April 1951; three days later, Albert
VI—along with eleven mice—became the first animals to survive
rocket flight, though Albert died two hours after his triumphal
return. Two of the mice also died—probably of heat exhaustion
while waiting in the New Mexico desert for their capsule to be
retrieved. Patricia and Mike, two cynomolgus monkeys, did survive their flight on 21 May 1952, but it was a short and low ride.
(Though none of these monkeys were called "George," it's relevant that all of them were given human names.) The transfor-
mative Soviet launch of a spaceship, *Sputnik,* would take place in
the year of this installment's publication, 1957. And it's clear that
H. A. Rey—who had a lifelong interest in astronomy—was committed to alerting his readership about the perils and pleasures
of space exploration; this book is *topical* in a way that the others
were not. The medal George earns when he comes back safely to
earth reads: "TO GEORGE; THE FIRST SPACE MONKEY."
The artist's audience by now is dealing with plausible contem-

porary headlines, not "Monkey Goes to Hospital" or "Monkey Hurt in Fall."

In the first book, the Man with the Yellow Hat returns to what looks like New York; in the second there's a skyscraper with many windows to wash. By the third installment the house they inhabit evokes small-town life (a lawn, a sidewalk, a paper route), and in *Curious George Gets a Medal,* there's a farm just down the road. Here the animals are domestic, not creatures in a zoo: there are goats and pigs and cows. Improbably enough, while escaping from farmers who chase him, George hops on a truck whose legend reads "Museum of Science" and soon enough arrives at a Museum—a Museum with dinosaurs on display in an exhibition hall resembling that of the Museum of Natural History in Manhattan. So the trip from farm to town is rapid: a turned page. We cut, as it were, to the chase.

By now the pattern is familiar, and the misadventures, though surprising, are to be expected. At book's start George is home alone; the doorbell rings; the mailman brings a letter. The "good little monkey" cannot read, but he is "always very curious," and though he cannot decipher the letter with his name on it he decides to try to write. He finds a pen; it's dry. He fills it with ink; the ink spills. The blue puddle on the floor will not respond to a blotter, so he decides to wash it out with water and soap powder because "that's what you clean up with!" He brings in a hose from the garden and sprays it on the soap; bubbles and lather "AND MORE LATHER" fill the room. George turns off the tap and fetches a shovel but by the time he returns to the room the lather has subsided and the floor looks like a lake of ink; he needs a pump instead.

In a promotional brochure composed for Houghton Mifflin, the authors report on this scene:

And where do the ideas come from? We wish we knew. Sometimes they don't come. Soaking in a hot bathtub—a news item in the papers—a piece of conversation at a party—

it all helps. Once we heard a biochemist tell how, as a boy, he had made a bargain with his mother to give the kitchen floor a thorough scrubbing in order to get money for a chemistry set. So one day while his parents were out, he sprinkled the contents of a large package of soap flakes on the floor, pulled the garden hose through the window and turned the water on. . . . In *Curious George Gets a Medal,* George emulates this experiment with spectacular results.

There's a kind of logic here, a step-by-step progression that leads from bad to worse. George runs down the road to a farm where he has seen a pump; it is too heavy to pull by himself, and so he tries to harness a goat in order to haul the machine. The goat bucks him away. He lands near a pen full of pigs and opens the gate so that one pig might help; instead the whole herd escapes. At last, George finds a cow to help him drag the pump and is riding happily back to his house when the farmer and his son—who have heard the squealing animals—rush in from fields and corral the pigs and give chase to what they see in the distance as their stolen cow and pump. To escape the angry farmers—the chase-motif, again—George hides in a laundry line, enveloped in a hanging shirt, then jumps on a passing truck that carries him to the museum. Inside, he stares at animals and, hungry, climbs up on a stuffed dinosaur to pull at a palm tree's coconuts. They too, we learn, are stuffed. In a scene reminiscent of *Bringing Up Baby,* where Cary Grant, teetering on a precious dinosaur skeleton, brings it down, George yanks at the nuts and the whole vast display comes undone.

"Guards came rushing in from all sides, and underneath the fallen dinosaur they found a little monkey!" The director of the museum, Professor Wiseman—note the name—is furious and tells the guards to put the vandal in a cage and take him to a zoo. In the nick of time, however, the Man with the Yellow Hat appears and brings George the letter with which the adventure began.

We see it reproduced. The letter turns out to have come from Professor Wiseman himself, asking George to volunteer for the space exploration that will make him yet more famous. The next pages picture preparations for space travel, liftoff and its attendant suspense, then the return and retrieval of the capsule. Everyone applauds the traveler—"even the farmer and his son, and the kind woman from next door" (who had worked for hours to get the water out of the room). All ends well.

George has volition here, and agency; once enrolled in the space program, he plays an important role. The imp and scamp and well-intentioned alien now manages a spaceship and lever and parachute, persuading all who watch him that it's possible "to come back to earth." This early astronaut is simian, but an astronaut nevertheless. From a creature home alone to someone chased by farmers and chastised by professors, he becomes a national hero. And the final image shows him smiling at his mirrored self and wearing a gold medal: "It was the happiest day in George's life."

(5) *Curious George Flies a Kite,* 1958

In this fifth installment we find ourselves again in suburbia or a semirural world. There are houses in fields, and lakes to fish in, and people who keep rabbits. Once again the Man with the Yellow Hat, in whose house George lives, drives off for the day and leaves the monkey alone. His cautionary warning, before he goes, is that George should behave and not be overcurious; we readers know in advance, of course, that this won't be the case.

A series of encounters follows. This book is longer than its predecessors and a touch formulaic; George moves from **A** to **B** to **C** in a predictable sequence; his "adventures" are new, but we guess where they're likely to lead. He starts the day by playing inside with a ball, doing tricks, and looking out a window to see a big house where Bill—whom we soon meet—lives. There's also a little house in a large walled garden; George climbs the wall and sees that the house is in actuality a rabbit hutch. He's learned, perhaps, from his experience with pigs in *Curious George Gets a Medal,* to be at least a little careful; he extracts only one baby bunny from the pen—and plays happily with his new friend until the bunny disappears. The monkey ponders this; he returns to the hutch, ties a piece of string around the mother rabbit, and the mother rabbit finds her child at the edge of the garden; all's well. They return to the hutch.

Next, and with his piece of string intact, George follows a plump fisherman and watches the man catch fish. He wants to do the same. Returning to his house, he takes a mop and hook and piece of cake and baits his line and goes fishing. He catches nothing, eats the cake, and then falls into the lake. (This is somewhat reminiscent of his plunge into the ocean in *Curious George,* but he's able to clamber out by himself, dripping wet.) His friend Bill arrives, carrying a kite, and promises to show George how high the kite can fly.

The monkey is delighted. They play. And when the kite gets stuck in a tree he climbs the trunk and "little by little he got the string out of the tree." It's growing late; Bill goes to fetch his bike, first telling George to stay with the kite and warning him not to let it fly away. Nonetheless, George lets "the string go a little, and then a little more . . ." until he's hoisted bodily into the air and rides high in the sky near the lake. A frightened Bill fetches the Man with the Yellow Hat, telling himself "the man would know what to do." Indeed, he does; he rushes off and finds a helicopter which he then pilots expertly, effecting a midair rescue of both George and the kite. (Never mind that a helicopter's blade would make mincemeat of kite and string; the adventure ends with everybody safe and all the equipment intact.) Bill is grateful and relieved to have his kite returned; he gives George a baby bunny for a pet. The final illustration has the monkey feeding his new friend a carrot on the yellow floorboards of his house; a toy giraffe (reminiscent of Rafi) stands against a wall.

These activities—ball-playing, fishing, flying a kite, keeping a pet—inhabit the domain of childhood, very much the sort of thing a boy or girl engages in during a charmed youth. The world of Curious George in the "original" texts is a world full of pitfalls and pratfalls but no actual threat. And whenever George *does* seem at risk, he's rescued by his friend. The Man with the Yellow Hat is nameless, often absent, but always, in the end, able to avert disaster and to save the day.

No one else recurs from book to book or provides a throughline in the seven stories. So his role here is worth pondering: Is he a benevolent despot, an oppositional presence, a guardian, a mage? His headgear and his yellow suit, his blue convertible, his appropriate equipment (a gun in the first installment, a helicopter in this one) all suggest a kind of mastery, but a gentle one. He's often confused as to George's whereabouts—"Where's George?" is a refrain on the order of the much-later "Where's Waldo?"—but supremely competent to fix what requires fixing. Always he makes a last-minute appearance, arriving to act as savior. And more and more we get the feeling he needs George as much as he is needed; there's reciprocity here.

By 1958, nearly twenty years after his first incarnation in the first book by the Reys (*Cecily G. and the Nine Monkeys* appeared in 1939), George has grown a trifle shopworn. His creators allowed themselves to pursue other interests; H. A. Rey published a book called *The Stars: A New Way to See Them* in 1952. His was a long-term fascination with astronomy—one that commenced as far back as his service as a soldier in World War I—and he "redrew" the constellations so as to make them more accessible to the naked eye. Wittily, and when releasing a simplified version of *The Stars* for children (*Find the Constellations*, 1954), he said the language was so spare and direct that even adults could make sense of it. The previous ascent of George in a spaceship is part and parcel of this interest; the monkey has, as it were, a bird's-eye view of the skies and therefore the earth below. An overarching theme in the books—and a source of their particular pleasure—is that George can manage what his readership cannot; a child can dream of aerial reconnaissance and of being rescued, but George enacts those dreams.

This holds true in all successful storytelling: the reader must empathize with a character and experience vicariously what the character feels and fears. But it's worth repeating that the character is a monkey, and the anthropomorphic balancing act is now in full swing. On a double-leaf page showing George "high as a kite," we read the following: "Not even a monkey can jump from the sky. George was scared. What if he never got back? Maybe he would fly on and on and on. Oh, he would never, never be so curious again, if just this one time he could find a way to get home."

Adjacent to this issue is the *kind* of fear he feels, the *kind* of opposition he encounters. There's no villain here. Unlike those cartoons or children's tales that have an active adversary, George wrestles with no demons but his own. And the demon—curiosity—is, in moderation, a virtue not a vice; the world the Reys bring into being on the page is a world without evil or genuine harm. Think of all those comic books or filmstrips where someone chases someone else, attempting to eat or enslave them; think of all those cliffhangers where the villain twirls his mustachio or grinds his teeth in rage. Even cartoon monsters have the power to intimidate, and most "adventure" stories suggest there's some real danger for the hero or the heroine to face. Bugs Bunny and Popeye the Sailor and Little Red Riding Hood and the rest all have their enemies; the majority of children's entertainments traffic in an at-least-momentary fear.

By contrast, these tales are benign. To continue with comparatives, the style of *Curious George* anticipates the mode of "Sesame Street" or "Mr. Rogers' Neighborhood"; it's meant to reassure, not terrify, its audience, and the trouble George gets into is of his own making. No one plots against him; no one tries to harm him; the worst that happens is a chase, and there's always a rescue at hand. So when George "was scared" and asks himself, "What if he never got back?" we watch without anxiety while the Man with the Yellow Hat engineers his safe return. This all may have something to do with the genuine evil of the Third Reich and the horror of the Holocaust; Hans and Margret Rey had known enough privation not to visit it on others. Their vision is a gentle one, and the "good little monkey" survives.

It overstates the point, perhaps, to say the intention of these stories is to heal, anneal, but children who read or watch Curious George don't feel themselves at risk. No terror here. George feeds his bunny at book's end, and everybody's home.

(6) *Curious George Learns the Alphabet,* 1963

This volume is frankly didactic. It offers instruction at least as much as entertainment; it's a primer for young readers who are beginning to read. The "adventure" is the alphabet, and the verb of the title feels central. The other five governing verbs of titles in the series—*takes, rides, gets, flies, goes*—are active ones, where increased awareness is a by-blow of the story line: *Don't paint on walls, Don't feed an ostrich, Don't let out the string of a kite.* This is not to reduce the previous books to a set of simple imperatives, but learning letters is a different mode of behavior than riding a bicycle or flying a kite, and the central action here is what the monkey *learns.* There are a few interruptions and secondary story lines, but the thrust of the whole is to teach George and there-fore his young auditor how to get from **A** to **Z**. Every word is a beginner-word; the language has been stripped.

Therefore, illustrations are central. More than any other entry in the series, this is a picture book. On the title page of *Curious George Learns the Alphabet* we watch George standing at an easel whose canvas is a blank white pad of paper waiting to be written on; he holds a brush as pen. On the last page of the story, he's sitting, eating doughnuts (with which he's learned to spell THE END) and turning illustrated pages; it seems he now can read. Every once in a while, the patient teacher allows his student a brief recess, a chance to absorb what he's learned. George tries to read; he tries to write; he gets to play football for a few minutes to work off excess energy; he goes to the baker for doughnuts. But there's nearly nothing in or about the surrounding community to serve as a distraction; we don't know, for instance, if we inhabit the countryside or live in a village or town. There's a brief encounter with a baker, who says that ten dozen doughnuts require a large bag, but that's the totality of interaction with anyone other than his friend, the Man with the Yellow Hat. And almost all the action takes place inside a room. By comparison with the other "adventures" the Reys imagined for Curious George, this is an interior journey and an uneventful one.

More precisely, the adventure and the series of events have to do with curiosity slaked. To start with, George stares uncomprehendingly at a stack of his friend's books. "They were full of little black marks and dots and lines, and George was curious—what could one do with them?"

By the end of the story, he knows. His first reaction has been to tear a book apart to try to find what's in it, but the Man with the Yellow Hat prevents any serious damage. Then—as a kind of stand-in for all authors—the man proclaims: "Books are full of stories. Stories are made of words, and words are made of letters. If you want to read a story you first have to know the letters of the alphabet. Let me show you."

And, for the rest of the book, he will. Each of the twenty-six letters gets at least two pages—one devoted to capital **A** and one to small **a**; one devoted to **B**, one to **b**; and so on. This offers H. A. Rey the chance to draw a bestiary; there are alligators, birds and bees, crabs and dinosaurs and dromedaries all the way through to a yak and a zebra. Not every illustration represents the animal kingdom (we see a **c**ab, a **h**ouse, an **i**cicle, etc.), but the majority of pictures do show animals, and at the bottom of the page a small George plays with or peers at them, acquiring basic English.

Most of us know the alphabet song, that simple tune with which we help children acquire the letters **A**, **B**, **C**, and more. But this is a visual version thereof, and it must be sounded out. Inventive and idiosyncratic, the illustrations show a Kangaroo with a body shaped by a brown **K**, a Jaguar with a spotted **J**, a Lion with a yellow **L** that shapes its torso, walking. Another original strategy has to do with iteration—an alliterative description of the picture on display. The legend under the big **L**, for example, reads: "is a Lion. He is LUCKY. He is going to have LEG of LAMB for LUNCH, and he LOVES it."

Each of the operative letters is colored to compel attention, so that the yellow Lion has a set of yellow **L**s beneath it, and the repetition of the letter drives its meaning home. "The big **G** is a GOOSE. GOOSE starts with a **G**, like GEORGE." Or: "The small **p** is a small penguin. These penguins live near the South Pole. They use their flappers as paddles. George knew penguins from the Zoo." This is verbal ingenuity that acts as a kind of repetitive and visual instruction; by the time the young reader has looked at eight *p*s in a row, the letter may well be retained.

So George grows literate in the course of the book—able to read, then write. This does not mean he learns to speak or that his nature will alter; he remains a playful creature who plays by his own rules. In the only developed incident or plot point of the story, he changes an order placed by the Man with the Yellow Hat from "one dozen doughnuts" to "ten." The surprised baker complies with the note, and George returns with an overflowing sack of doughnuts—spilling them out on the table, then the floor.

His friend is shocked, then sees the note where George has written TEN. Philosophical, he says, "Well, that comes from teaching the alphabet to a little monkey. And I told you: no tricks!" This brings to mind, though distantly, William Shakespeare's great final play, *The Tempest.* The magician Prospero and his servant Caliban are only faintly present here, but present nonetheless. In act 1, scene 2, Caliban (an anagram for "cannibal") rears up and tells his master, "You taught me language, and my profit on't / is I know how to curse." Elsewhere he describes his fear of "apes with foreheads villainous low," and Caliban has of course a very different nature from that of Curious George.

But George's "profit on't" is an additional nine dozen doughnuts, and the Man with the Yellow Hat admits "that comes from teaching the alphabet to a little monkey."

It's fair to say this book relies on its five predecessors in order to be effective; I doubt that a young reader, coming cold to *Curious George Learns the Alphabet,* would understand the subtext of the text. With the exception of the incident described above, George is largely passive, a witness to the letters and their pictorial representation page by page. Neither he nor the Man with the Yellow Hat engages in complicated action or find themselves at risk; there's neither a chase nor an aerial exploit, no bear requiring rescue from a tree. And though there are of course many ways a child acquires literacy—many modes and habits of instruction—this volume describes a learning curve; from someone trying to decipher the black marks upon a page, George and his audience will learn what letters mean. By the end of this sixth installment, *The Adventures of Curious George* includes an exploration of language, which our hero can manipulate to his own advantage. The images are each an *aide-memoire.*

To me, at least, this volume is qualitatively different from the others in one crucial way. It has a kind of authority, a sense of the importance of its established characters. There's the feel of franchise, of a recognizable pattern, and what goes on between the student and the teacher—the monkey and the Man with the Yellow Hat—depends upon their prior history. It requires less explaining; it's where we've been before. When we see the letter **M** and meet Mister Miller, the Mailman, the letter he brings ("Maybe it's for ME, thinks George") is reminiscent of the letter sent in *Curious George Gets a Medal.* And when in **V** for Valentine, George gets a letter sent with love from the Man with the Yellow Hat, we're told in lowercase that "George loved valentines. He got several valentine cards every year. One card came from Nevada." No doubt on Valentine's Day, thereafter—I have reprinted some such examples—George received packets of mail.

(7) *Curious George Goes to the Hospital,* 1966

Here the feel of an established franchise is even more pronounced. A quarter of a century after his first publication, George needs no introduction (though the formulaic first line "This is George" continues to apply.) He's familiar to his audience—who may well be introducing him to their own young children. Indeed, while in the hospital waiting room, he's recognized by one of the mothers: "'Look, Betsy,' the woman next to him said to her little girl, 'there is Curious George!'" (As an aside, and perhaps a private joke, the two first names *other* than George we encounter in the prior volumes—Bob and Bill—each begin with **B**. Here, we meet Betsy "in bed looking sad.") There are additional people (and further first letters) on the ward, including Dave, who "was having a blood transfusion," and Steve, who "had his leg bandaged and was sitting in a go-cart." His youthful fellow-patients—with the exception of silent, frightened Betsy—all seem pleased to be in George's presence. He's a celebrity now.

The book begins with a gift. The Man with the Yellow Hat gives a jigsaw puzzle to George; they piece it together and discover, just short of completion, that one of the pieces is lost. The puzzle itself is an image of a monkey in a jungle, being curious and approaching a large yellow hat—referencing, of course, the first episode of *Curious George.* When our hero wakes up the next day with a stomachache, it takes no great deductive prowess to know that the missing puzzle piece has been engorged. The rest of the story that follows deals with the aftermath of that accidental swallowing, and the dénouement takes its time. There are fewer venues, fewer incidents, and much more to be *learned.*

Underneath the title, we're told the book has been produced "In Collaboration With the Children's Hospital Medical Center, Boston." Like its predecessor, this volume is didactic: explicitly so. The mode is representational, and the implicit purpose is to render a visit to a hospital less frightening to children. There's nothing fearsome in the drawings (imagine if the book were illustrated instead by Maurice Sendak or Edward Gorey), and the information provided is easy to "digest." We learn about the barium a patient drinks, the lead aprons technicians must wear while using the X-ray machine, the bracelet with his name on it George needs to strap to his wrist. We watch him have his temperature taken, then watch him take a pill and fight to stay awake, for "he was curious to see what would happen next." We watch him shy away from a needle, then discover the inoculation "really was not" so bad. We meet a "pretty nurse" called Carol; we meet kind Doctor Baker "who had been to the house when it all had started," and finally—having been anesthetized—the patient falls asleep.

When George wakes up, the operation's over, and it has been a success. He's told they have removed the offending puzzle-piece from his stomach and that in a day or two he'll be just fine. He must allow himself to sleep and heal, but—as with all his previous imbroglios—the problem has been solved. (It's true, of course, that a small piece of a cardboard puzzle is not likely to have caused so large an upheaval in George's intestinal tract, but we as readers wouldn't want a genuinely threatful malady; the illness here is manageable and a one-time thing. The Reys succeed in stripping these hospital transactions and procedures of their power to alarm.)

Social context has expanded. In *Curious George Learns the Alphabet,* as we have seen, it's two friends alone in a room; here, the cast is large. And for the first time the pictures show women: a pretty nurse, a fellow-patient. With few exceptions—such as the irate owner of the apartment George paints in *Curious George Takes a Job*—the secondary characters in the stories have been male. Here the ward hosts boys and girls in almost equal measure—though it has, of course, only one monkey. There's an important female presence in this installment: young Betsy, who is sad when we meet her in the waiting room. She watches George intently, refusing to grin, sleeping in an adjacent bed and inconsolable. (George too cries when left alone for the night; the hospital is not a wholly happy place.) Little by little, however, the girl grows better humored, learning to finger paint, watching a puppet show performed by the agile patient with "four hands," and smiling when George falls off a merry-go-round he constructed from a record player. Then he goes for a ride in the abandoned go-cart and loses control of it, driving, slamming full-tilt into a group of dignitaries visiting the hospital. Cups and plates are broken; cutlery is scattered; food spills. When George has his accident, making a huge mess of the service trays and startling the dark-suited Mayor, Betsy bursts out laughing and is cured.

She comforts the monkey, telling him not to be sad. "The whole thing was SO funny! I never laughed so much in my life. I'm so glad you were in the hospital with me." The director of the hospital forgives him for the "terrible mess" because, as he puts it, George has brought a healing merriment to others in the room. "'But you also made our sad little Betsy happy again, and that is more than any of us have done." There's a cue here, clearly, for sick children: be lighthearted, unafraid.

It's worth remembering, at series' end, how much ground has been traversed. At the completion of this story, George receives a second present from Nurse Carol—a smaller package than the box with the puzzle that began this episode. Once home again, he rips open "the box—and THERE was the piece of the puzzle that had caused all the trouble!" The doctor has saved and returned it; it's heart-shaped and light green. "And NOW we can finish the puzzle," says the Man with the Yellow Hat, preparing to insert the final piece in the green jungle where the monkey examines—curiously—the very hat with which he was entranced and entrapped at the start of the seven installments, a quarter of a century before. Again, what had been lost is found; again, peace is restored.

The circularity of such a structure—and the self-reflexive nature of the illustrations (a picture of George on the wall, a picture of George in a puzzle, a jungle George paints in an apartment, with a self-portrait climbing a palm tree)—reinforces the idea of order in a disorderly world. Too, the repetitive pattern—

curiosity, chaos, disaster averted—satisfies young readers; they don't know what will happen but they know what to expect. And though Hans and Margret Rey were surely unaware, when they stuffed the prototype of *Curious George* into the bags of the bicycles they rode out of Paris, that theirs would an enduring success, the ingredients of that success were with them from the start. George is a "good little monkey"; what ails him can be cured.

*

```
Mr. H. A. Rey:
Dear Sir:
I like the book Curious George very much. The
best part off all was When he called the Fire
department. And when he whent to prison.
yours truly, Roger Hamilton
[Spelling errors retained.]
```

*

The pair were constantly productive; their archive in the de Grummond Collection of Children's Literature at the University of South Mississippi in Hattiesburg bulks large. In the more than three hundred cardboard containers, ranging from small to sizable, there are photographs and posters, pieces of Margret's pottery and drawings of the solar system and outlines of the History of the World, with epoch after epoch illustrated and described. A set of three-foot-long cartons is devoted to *Road Atlas of the Sky.* Racked and stacked on the library shelves, there's a box containing Indian Tortoise Stories, one called Evolution of the Animals, one begun but not completed by Margret, called Gardening by an Ignoramus, which Hans planned to illustrate. There's a book called *The Cigar Tree, or How the Tobacco Plant Came into Being—A Mythical Story, Mainly for Men.* There are hand puppets and dolls. One carton contains an advertisement for XYRENE after shaving lotion: *Après la barbe, le visage en feu?* ["After shaving, is your face on fire?"], and the poster shows a bald man with a downcast expression, a flaming cheek, a hand cupping his sore chin. There are picture books that were never produced and many mock-ups of those that were. There are boxes of letters between husband and wife, composed when she was elsewhere—at an art colony in Maine, at their cottage in New Hampshire—filled with details of their daily life. To describe the whole of the archive would double the size of this text.

Although their output was a large one, the rate of production was slow. As they wrote for Houghton Mifflin, "One thing is clear, though: doing a book is hard work for us. People sometimes think we dash them off. We wish we could. We work very long on each one, frequently over a year. We write and rewrite, we draw and redraw, we fight over the plot, the beginning, the ending, the illustrations—as a matter of fact our work is nearly the only thing we do fight about."

While the quality can vary, what strikes one is the quantity, the ongoing inventiveness. In a certain sense the Reys—many years before the genre grew commercial—understood the future of illustrated books. Their images go hand-in-hand with story line; although their chosen audience is a young one, the "adventures" presage by decades the present vogue of graphic novels. With a near-obsessive passion, Hans drew and drew and drew.

And he loved language also, the cacophony of sounds words make as they supplant each other. Here are a few of his illustrated rhymes:

In India lived once a Fakir
Who buried a watch on his acre
The harvest next fall,
was 12 watches in all
which he sold to his friend the watch maker.

[Here the illustration shows a bearded fakir with a twelve watches on the branches of a tree.]

There was a cute agouty
which had been put on duty
as chimney sweep
which made him weep
because he got so sooty.

[Here the illustration shows an agouti straddling a chimney
and wielding a broom on the roof. In the alphabet-couplets
to follow, the images are self-evident, and I confine myself to
reproducing a few of Rey's doggerel rhymes.]

Yesterday poor little Andy
ate two pounds of sugar candy
that was more than he could stand, he
looks and feels extremely bendy.

The owl in great despair
sits on the rocking chair
it tried to chase the rabbit
but was unable to grab it.

The toothbrush of the elephant
has fifteen hundred bristles
the haft is made of adamant
and when he's thru, he whistles.

The octopus
can't take the bus
His baggage is
too numerous

A snail tried to assail the U.S. mail
and was put in jail.

With a flat hat
and spats and cravat
the bat acts as an acrobat

On the Cape of Good Hope
Stands an Antelope
And stares at the stars through
a telescope

One hot night an Alligator
slept in a refrigerator
where his friends next morning found him
with a cube of ice around him.

I want to reduce
says Larry the Moose,
That's why I'm keen
on Lemon juice.

*

The fan mail continued. As if to demonstrate the adage that art is long and life is short, this letter was postmarked in Plattsburgh, NY, on 20 April 1982, a full five years after Rey's death:

Dear H. A. Rey. I love your books especially curious George goes to the hospital. And I have a stuff animal like curious George. And how are you doing I'm fine. And how was your easter myn was fine. And can I have a picture of you please. Thank you your friend Jennifer Bruso
[Spelling errors retained.]

*

The last time I saw Margret Rey was near the end of her days; my father (her compatriot from Hamburg) and I visited her at home on 14 Hilliard Street in Cambridge, Massachusetts. She had had an operation and was slowed, a little, though sitting still was no more congenial to Margret in her late eighties than is immobility to her famous brainchild. Curious George loomed everywhere: from a six-inch Gund version of the animal beside her on the couch to a five-foot-tall stuffed monkey wrapped around the banister.

Although I can't pretend to intimacy with the Reys, their cultural "surround" was and is familiar. We spoke of home, of old friends dead or dying, of *Max und Moritz*, the German antecedent of the Katzenjammer twins. She and her husband had attended my younger brother Andrew's wedding, and we remembered Hans's toast, that here were gathered "a rare group of Hamburgers." The house sat directly across from the Loeb Drama Center, where I had spent my student days and where my daughter, that evening, was going to perform. I was in my fifties then, but still her little Nicky gazing at the fireplace and hoping for a second helping of tea cake from the tray . . .

I did have questions I do want to ask. Consider this a piece of fan mail until now undelivered:

Dear Mr. and Mrs. Rey,

    Why did you wait so long to leave Paris; what made you think you were safe?

    Those bicycles you built and escaped on; any trace?

    Were there night-sweats, terror, the image of pursuing soldiers while you slept in barns?

    Many of the letters children sent you inquired about gender; they ask if you're a man or woman, which? Is the author's identity hidden or shared; did you use initials as a shield?

    To follow the books' titular credits (first H. A. Rey, then H. A. and Margret Rey, then Margret Rey, then Margret and H. A. Rey) is to track a power dynamic. Who were you when "at home"?

Your address book is chock-a-block with names of business associates and building contractors and doctors and friends (including those of my uncle, my parents, my brothers); when the word "home" sprang to mind, what was its location?

You gave your considerable archive to a university you'd never visited and a place you never traveled to—Hattiesburg, Mississippi. Why?

Did you ever consider returning to Hamburg or, as citizens of Brazil, settling there once more?

You both were outraged by the bombing in Vietnam and Laos and Cambodia; you were militant on civil rights and ardent social activists. Were you aggrieved by "Amerika," or did the Statue of Liberty's torch maintain its welcome flame?

The apartments in New York, the cottage in Waterville, the large house on Hilliard Street. The gardens, the anti-Bauhaus clutter, the love of open skies. Satisfaction, dissatisfaction? An asperity to Margret, a sweetness to the dying H. A. Rey.

At the end of her life, apparently, Margret planned large charitable donations to Israel, hoping to better the lives of the Jews. Was that a form of religious renewal; did it feel like a debt discharged?

Did Hans feel that his drawing skills were adequate, his sense of color instructed? As an autodidact, did he feel his wife was better trained, and did that impinge on his art?

Margret was, in the technical sense, a dilettante—with fixed but changeable focus, adept at several crafts and trades. Was that a disappointment or a delight?

You two were childless. Did you hope or plan
for family; did you try to have a child? And in
what ways did the inquisitive monkey play that
particular role?

A cocker spaniel, often, in the pages of the
books—and, always, one at home. When you imitated
lions, Hans, how loud was the roar?

Some of your commitments—to wind power, solar
energy, not to mention full racial equality—have
not as yet been realized. Was there frustration
involved?

For a quarter of a century you wrote books
together on *Curious George*; by 1966 you ceased
expanding the series and turned elsewhere. Why?

*

Dear George
Monkeys are my favorite animal
cuss I love to clime.
Why don't you name the
man with the yellow
hat. Why don't you have a tiale
your friend Katie.
[Spokane, Washington 18 September 1992. Spelling
errors retained.]

*

It seems to me, perhaps subjectively, that there's a European fla-
vor to the early illustrations; the streets and clothes and houses
resemble those portrayed by Ludwig Bemelmans or Antoine de
St. Éxupery. The purples and browns and blues evoke Paris as
much as New York. Slowly the colors and gardens change, the
accent falls *here* and not *there.* By the time of his full-fledged
licensed proliferation, George belongs to the United States, and
in the television series now there's no least doubt as to which

continent he inhabits. Indeed, the omnipresent monkey—with his contracts and distribution agreements—has become proof positive of the American dream. (The caliber of the recent children's books and television episodes is, to this reader and viewer, markedly inferior to the Reys' original efforts, but perhaps that's an unavoidable side effect of a commercial franchise produced for a mass audience.) On the screen of a Manhattan taxicab I took yesterday—that loop of news and advertising which greets every passenger—George floated upside down above Times Square.

Still, he remains a foreigner. This may have to do with the sense of strangeness attached to a "good little monkey": Does he or doesn't he *belong*? In Joseph Conrad's famous phrase, is he "one of us"? In Laurent de Brunhoff's Babar books, the creatures are by and large animal; there's scant crisscrossing interaction with the human race. By contrast, the "ape-man" Tarzan—that earlier creation of Edgar Rice Burroughs—appears as much at home on Savile Row as naked in a treetop, and much of his experience is intended as a commentary on the morals and the mores of civilization itself. More recently, the figure ET shows some of the same attributes—an extraterrestrial witness to and contrapuntal example of the way humans behave.

Domestication matters here; each narrative of man and beast describes the interaction of the two, and if a creature is intrinsically wild, the happy ending of such stories consists of staged reentry into wilderness. Elsa the Lioness gets "set free"; so does the Roman Androcles, once the lion he has befriended refuses to attack him in the Coliseum.

But man and dog or man and horse have different narrative arcs; if a creature is domestic, he/she remains that way. The bonds between trainer and animal trained may slip in the course of an action, but never entirely fray. We use "little monkey"—not "little snake" or "little shark"—as a term of parental endearment. In any case, George "translates" well, and it's perhaps not an accident that his first incarnation—as Fifi, one of *les neufs singes*—needs translation from the French. That group of monkeys seems a model of interactive decency: all nine of them work in concert, all travel in a pack.

Yet once George enters civilization, he doesn't miss or mourn his brothers and sisters back home. Perhaps his wordlessness derives from time spent in the African jungle, before he was adopted; he can learn to read and write but never, quite, to speak. In this regard such strangeness cuts both ways; George is no obvious candidate for domesticity (easy to housebreak? taught not to bite?), but he happily yields up wildness for the creature comforts offered by his friend. Our hero deals with other animals—giraffes, bears, ostriches, cows, pigs, and goats—throughout his adventures, but not with other monkeys; that might pose a challenge and cut over-close to the bone.

In the majority of children's "classics," there's a group dynamic at work. There are good or bad men and women, tame animals or fierce ones, and the interaction of particular members of opposing species itself provides a subject. Statler and Hilton of *Sesame Street* criticize the show put on by Kermit the Frog or Miss Piggy; in E. B. White's *Charlotte's Web,* farmers fatten pigs for slaughter; in Beatrix Potter's *Peter Rabbit,* they want to keep a rabbit from a vegetable patch. In *Paddington,* much of the story line (and film) considers how the orphaned bear can or will become a member of the human clan.

But George has no further commerce with his relatives from the first book: "Mother Pamplemoose and Baby Jinny, James who was good, Johnny who was brave, Arthur who was kind, David who was strong, and Punch and Judy, the twins." His society is that of *Homo sapiens*; in the first of the installments he leaves the jungle behind, in the second he leaves the zoo. And from then on out his loyalty is undivided: he won't go home again.

What his story amounts to is, in effect, a sermon on cooperation between species closely related but not quite the same. The Man with the Yellow Hat and Curious George endure brief separations but remain joined at the hip. They are symbiotic as well as sympathetic: indissolubly a pair. I've written at such length about a set of children's books because they seem to me a paradigm of our shared society; how to accommodate "the other" is a central thematic concern.

This may in part explain the animal's enduring charm; he cannot control his "curious" nature but tries hard to do so. When he fails he is forgiven; when he succeeds it's to applause and a collective relief. The Reys were passionate participants in the Civil Rights Movement of the 1960s, and the deep thematic message of *Curious George* is "We Shall Overcome." Our hero has done so, is doing so, and will continue to do so in every text and every theatrical and television show. His face in repose wears a smile.

N.B. In this essay the description of the Reys' flight from Paris derives in part from *The Journey That Saved Curious George: The True Wartime Escape of Margret and H. A. Rey,* Louise Borden, with illustrations by Allan Drummond (New York: Houghton Mifflin Harcourt, 2005).

The quotations and page references for the seven volumes of *Curious George* come from *The Complete Adventures of Curious George, 70th Anniversary Edition,* Margret and H. A. Rey, (New York: Houghton Mifflin Harcourt, 2011). All quotes derive from that text.

This is not a scholarly article, and I see no need to include the usual scholarly apparatus of full citations and footnotes. But there's a central source I must thank for this walk—or should I say bike ride?—down Memory Lane. The vast bulk of referents here (the letters from children, the Reys' brief autobiographical statements, the licensing agreements, Hans's doggerel rhymes, etc.) come from the archive of the H. A. & Margret Rey Papers, housed in the de Grummond Children's Literature Collection in the University of Southern Mississippi, Hattiesburg. I owe a debt of gratitude for the warm welcome extended by all the generous folk in the Children's Literature Collection, and particularly by its curator, Ellen Ruffin. She and the library staff made my stay happy as well as productive; the good humor of the Reys pervades the building's halls. Ema Ryan Yamazaki, the documentary filmmaker, and Lay Lee Ong, the executor of the Rey estate, have both been instructive and kind.

My Old Young Books

(*Possession, Sherbrookes, Stillness*)

I was born in England, of parents born in Germany, with an Italian name. It's a not uncommon story in this nation full of immigrants; mobility seems less the exception than rule. People move. We came to America when I was six; I have remained here since.

In my youth and young manhood, however, I traveled a good deal. The places my fictive family's scion, Ian Sherbrooke, visits—Iran, Afghanistan, Nepal—were stamped in my passport as well. My early books convey a wanderer's delight in distance; the first novel took place in Greece, the second more or less everywhere/nowhere, and the novel that preceded the Sherbrookes trilogy was set in the south of France.

At the age of twenty-four, I moved to southwestern Vermont. There, teaching at Bennington College, I fell under the spell of the landscape and dreamed a deep-rooted dream. Instead of change, I came to value constancy; instead of geographical variety, I wanted to write about those who stay put. Staring up at the Green Mountains, I grew vegetables and a beard, learned to ski and rototill, and began to think myself, if not a native, at least sufficiently immersed in it to focus on a novel of New England. I still can remember, and clearly, the day I decided to try.

It was 1975. I had joined the faculty of Bennington in 1966
and would remain there for ten further years. My wife and I were
living in a farmhouse on the grounds of the Park-McCullough
house, a large and imposing Victorian structure in the village
of North Bennington. I walked the trails and meadows daily
and knew the property well. At a certain point on one of those
walks—a fork in the road in a wood, as it happens, with a gate
overlooking a pasture—I understood *this* was the place I had
come to call home, not Greece or France or London or New York
or Timbuktu. I can remember telling myself there was no point
pretending otherwise; I was an American writer and needed
to set a book *here*. Before all else, therefore, I knew my novel's
location; it came prior to the story line or characters or any
conflict between them. And since I knew the owner of the Park-
McCullough mansion, I asked his permission to use the locale.

He gave it. His family had been retentive; they kept laundry lists and letters and records of business transactions from the
nineteenth century, and he provided me with access to an attic
full of documents. There were thousands of pages in boxes; I
read and read. At some point in that process, however, I came to
understand that these figures from the distant and the recent past
failed to fire my imagination; they seemed—not to put too fine
a point upon it—dull. To the degree that the three books of the
Sherbrookes trilogy are historical novels (as in the letters of Peacock Sherbrooke, his daughter, and his grandson), early research
may have left its residue, but the generations of my family are
each and all invented. So I began with paired imperatives: use the
landscape of southwestern Vermont, and people it with people
who have been made up.

Here is how I put it in a prefatory note to the first of the volumes, *Possession*:

> The author wishes to thank John G. McCullough for his gen-
> erosity in making available the files of the Park-McCullough
> House. The location of this novel more or less accurately
> describes the locus of that house—but I wish to make it clear

that the characters within it are wholly invented, not real. It would be a poor return for kindness indeed if any reader were to confuse my imaginary Sherbrooke tribe with the residents of the Governor McCullough Mansion, present or past.

I would like, in the pages that follow, to provide a kind of gloss on what I believed I was doing and what I believe I have done. The Sherbrookes trilogy (*Possession*, 1977; *Sherbrookes*, 1978; *Stillness*, 1980) was a major project for me and, though I'd published seven previous books, felt like the end of a learning curve. When the third of those three texts was done, I had cut my eye-teeth as a novelist and was no longer a beginner. It's simple truth, not boastful, to say those books were widely reviewed and well received; by 1980 I could fairly claim to have finished my apprenticeship and entered into the guild. Yet more or less coeval with completion of the trilogy, I lost my bearings in the longer form and would not publish a novel again for fifteen years.

So the opportunity to reconsider these old efforts is a welcome one. For openers, I'm now much closer in age to the seventy-six-year-old Judah Sherbrooke, the protagonist of *Possession*, than to the age of the writer who invented him; from my present vantage it has been astonishing to see how much I knew then and how much I failed to know. The British boy who impersonated a Greco-American and resident of Southern France next borrowed the garb of Yankee settlers and the accents of New England. But what was I up to, and why?

*

When John O'Brien (the publisher of Dalkey Archive Press) kindly offered to bring the trilogy back to print-life, there was a choice to make. Most authors, including this one earlier, are glad for the chance to reissue old texts and leave well enough alone. At worst, the errors of juvenilia are simply that: one fixes a comma or adds a footnote and the book exists anew. It's a record of a time and place, not something one should tamper with. Painters and composers often revisit their previous work and offer, as it were, variations on a theme. Some authors—famously Henry James in the New York Edition of 1909 or, more recently, Peter Matthiessen in his rewritten trilogy—do undertake a full-fledged overhaul of what they wrote before. But the majority of writers seem content to say, *Here. What's done is done.*

In my case, however, the three books were one, and I had conceived them as such. The structure of *Possession,* for example, mirrors that of *Stillness*—with *Sherbrookes* as a kind of second movement and pastoral interlude. The first and third books' actions transpire in a single day; the second deals with gestation and plays out over months. The seventy-six-year-old Judah whom we meet on page 1 has his birth attested to by a doting father at the end of book 3. All along I'd hoped to publish them as a single volume, or a kind of triptych, and when I was invited to do so it seemed the right way to proceed.

Yet certain issues if not problems came immediately clear. First, volumes two and three contained passages of recapitulation—in order to tell a new reader what happened in previous texts. (Judah dies in the interstices of *Possession* and its sequel, *Sherbrookes*; his sister Harriet drowns herself at the end of the second installment, and the reader of the third book, *Stillness,* would have to be aware of this. Secondary characters such as Samson Finney and Lucy Gregory make what seems like a debut appearance in *Stillness,* but have in fact been introduced some hundreds of pages before.) These repetitions felt redundant and could be edited out. This I did. But once I began with red pencil and scissors, I found it hard to cease cutting; the entire text—sentence by sentence and paragraph by page—could be, it seemed to me, pruned. In the aggregate I cut roughly seven percent of the whole: nearly ten percent of *Possession* and less of the subsequent two installments. The book now comprises some 200,000 words—a long novel by any reckoning but not, I hope, bloat.

The simplest way to put it is this: I changed nothing important in *Sherbrookes*—retaining the second book's title as the title of all three. I added nothing of note. The characters and conflict and action and tone remain the same. The thematic matter (of which more later) is constant, as is the order of scenes. But no single page of prose escaped my editorial intervention; I'd written the sentences long ago and could rewrite them now. Why not, I asked myself, improve what needed improving; why leave a phrase intact when it could be with profit rephrased? The good news is—or so I told myself—that I'm a better writer now than when I started *Possession*. The bad news is the same. The youthful exuberance of Delbanco's prose troubled the older Delbanco, who has learned to admire restraint. Someday perhaps some scrupulous someone may compare the trilogy with this single volume, but at the present moment I'm the "sole proprietor" of the territory of *Sherbrookes* and can alter its property lines.

*

A few examples may suffice of what and how I revised. I bowdlerized the text a little and simplified it a lot. Some of this was a necessary consequence of present-day technology. My books were composed on a typewriter, not a computer, and no previous word-document exists. So the pages all had to be scanned. That process has become increasingly precise, but there were many errors of transmission—"lit" for "hit" and "nickering" for "flickering" and, routinely, "r" and "n" conjoined as "rn" where the original letter was "m." Some passages were missing; others were reproduced twice. In effect, I was required to copyedit *Sherbrookes* more than thirty years after it came into print, and I worked my way through the three volumes with a proofreader's eye. Having done so, now, at length, I feel more or less confident of exactness—but in the process of such tinkering I could not keep from changing words as well as correcting their spelling: from fixing, as it were, the language as well as the text.

For example, I substituted "the day after Judah's funeral" for "ten days after Judah's death," when Ian calls his mother at the beginning of *Sherbrookes*. It seemed wrong for him to wait the longer period; he was conflicted over his duty to his dead father, not to his living mother. This is a small editorial intervention only, but it does register change. And I cut the last line of *Sherbrookes*, since it seemed over-explicit; we do not need, as readers, to be told: "They huddle together, as once they would with Judah, and are well."

The process of revision could be as simple as the substitution of "She said she'll write you it's her own idea to come" for the original "She said she'll write you that it's her idea to come." Or the alteration of the phrase "not to waste this time" to "not to enjoy this time"; the word *waste* seemed less clear than *enjoy*. Or the substitution of "with glass and gauze between them" for "with glass and gauze intervening." I did try to fine-tune a character's diction: "Who knows your reasons, lady?" becomes, in Hattie's voice, "Who knows your reasons, missy?"

To this older writer's eye the younger writer over-ascribed dialogue; I cut perhaps a hundred usages of "he said" and "she said." These had been more a function of rhythm than necessity; in the first published version I used "he said" and "she said" as taglines throughout the spoken discourse, and they could be—with no loss of clarity—removed. At that period I had (still have, no doubt) an excessive fondness for semicolons and that often-needless word *that*. Too, I used to love to turn nouns into adjectives by means of a hyphen; this seemed a habit to break. So by using an added conjunction I could substitute the phrase "comfort and temptation," for the invented compound-word "comfort-temptation." To my present ear, this seems an improvement and slightly less mannerist prose.

Repetition is another habit I did try to break. When, for example, I had Judah both "triumphant" and "triumphing" in a single page of text I cut the former usage. And sometimes I would cut a phrase I liked because it called too much attention to itself: "the farthest twig of the outermost branch of Sullivanian analysis," became "the farthest wing of the renegade branch"—which is more accurate as a description if less engaging as trope.

The bulk of what I excised was sheer rhetorical excess. I was too fond of metaphor and the abstract generality—or so I now believe. William Faulkner and Malcolm Lowry were my masters then; these days I'm more committed to power in reserve. A phrase such as the following seemed a candidate for cutting, with nothing but verbiage lost: "the past is as the present's shadow, shortening and lengthening and mutable in the terms of perspective, changing with sightlines or on hillsides or pavement or light—yet truly immutable, fixed."

Or, "He is haunted by flesh, not fleshlessness, and he twined his limbs' decrepitude around his young wife's limbs. She does not fade or stale; she took lovers twenty years her junior, as he had taken her. She tempts him now continually, even in decrepitude, and is not dead but quick."

*

For the adept of variora, here are some examples of what has been cut:

> There are those who train with horseshoes and can throw and ring the horseshoes as part of their performance. There are those, Maggie knows, who can drop one orange or Indian club yet not break their juggling rhythm. Some jugglers can stack cups on saucers without shattering the cups. She herself is more agile than most; she has kept a close inventory of relatives and lovers and the patterned arc they make, from throwing hand to catching hand, suspended.

> He cannot remember her out of the wind, now Judah comes to think of it, or ever less than airy light for all the years' stiffening additions—and remembers now the nursery rhyme about the oak tree near the ocean, and reeds: how everything is leveled in the last big wind but bending reeds, how roots and all mean nothing when the hurricane and thunder come.

> So she kept *doing* and *talking* aloft. Things hung there suspended an instant, in perfect opposition to the force of grav-

ity—only rotating, not rising or falling, and for that perfected
instant she could keep three men convinced they were her only
man, or persuade two aunts in the same room that they were
her favorite aunt. At such times, she told herself, she could persuade a Catholic with seven children to embrace the right to
choose, or vote for George McGovern since he'd bring the boys
back home.

Ian would be staring at the traces of a lesson-plan, trying to learn
what he needed to know—while there was only her blurred
mouthing, only the spoor of the sentence she'd thought and
no blackboard and no chalk and nobody there to nudge him
with the answer. Still, he picked it up. He lip-read, thought-
read, read without reading; if only he'd been half the student
in school that he'd been of her manners' schooling, Hattie said,
why then he'd be adept at fractions and geography and pen-
manship also. He learned degree and size.

She yearned for him. She was, she told herself, in love. It wasn't
a term she much liked. It was attended by guitars. It had meant
crush—some hero's sock stolen from the basketball court, and
treasured, rolled into a totem in her top right drawer. Later
it meant four-leaf clovers proffered as they walked through
fields, and later the wine bottles shared. So love became a paw-
ing intensity—and the terms were making out, then making it,
then making love. Later still it meant submission. It meant Bil-
lie Holiday singing "Hush Now, Don't Explain"—the whiskey
seams in her voice come unstuck, a fiddler using nerve and hair
ends for her strings.

It's not as though these passages strike me as poorly written—just that they seem excessive and at least a little ponderous.
I was flexing verbal muscles then that now seem over-exercised;
my guiding principle throughout the revision was, in effect,
"Less is more." In several instances (particularly from *Possession*)

I excised entire scenes. I cut, for example, memories of Judah's grandmother, of Ian's escapades abroad, and Maggie's trip to Los Angeles since they failed to advance the tale's action—or were a gravitational side-drag upon it. Dialogue, too, went on too long, and I cut exchanges that seemed merely to mark time:

"That's nice," she said. "That's complimentary."

"It's the way I meant it."

"Men do yoga too. The world's best athlete is a ballet dancer."

"Who says?"

"*Time* magazine," she said. "And they must be right."

"I didn't call it sissy work. Just woman's."

So, to spite him, she had kept at it. She taught Ian to sit in the lotus position.

"Judah"—she would summon him—"what kind of tree is that?"

"A birch tree, grandma."

"Yes. What kind of birch?"

"A silver birch."

"What other kind would it be?"

"A silver bitch," he'd mutter, and she strained to hear.

"What?"

"A white birch maybe, but it isn't. It's a silver birch."

She'd have her notebook out, and wet the pencil stub.

"Beech, did you say beech?"

"No."

"Hattie knows the answer. She could tell."

He put his hands in his pockets. He balled his fingers to fists.

"Fess up, Judah, you said beech—that's a penny less this morning. That cancels out the elm."

"*Birch,* I said. Silver birch."

"You got the popple," she would say. "You got the cottonwood."

"Do it again," he'd ask her.

"Why?"

"It's fine to watch."

So she'd pick the limp lengths up again and turn her back to him and work her arms and then turn back with magic entanglements, fanning out and in. He wanted her to try with tinsel, but it wasn't long or strong enough. So he fashioned her, one Christmas, a tinsel necklace and bracelet and earrings and said, "They'll hold. You wear them," and she was his glittering creature lit by the Christmas tree lights. They made daisy chains from Reynolds Wrap, and Maggie said, "Imagine. There's country where it's warm enough so you can find real daisies in December." He imagined that.

*

I began with the assertion that I'd always thought of three as one; that is not quite the case. When I first tried to people the landscape of North Bennington, I started with a phrase—or, more precisely, tableau. For some time I had been thinking of the story of King David, and the great biblical description of that warrior-poet's old age. Fading, cold, and failing, he is offered the company of Abishag the Shunammite in his tent at night. But her body's warmth cannot rouse him. The Old Testament's indelible description reads: "And the damsel was very fair, and cherished the king, and ministered to him: but the king knew her not" (I Kings 4). That last phrase engendered *Possession* and remains embedded in it still.

More generally, I had the image of a funeral pyre erected at a tribal hero's death. This is the sort of practice collectively attested to in Norse mythology, Anglo-Saxon legend, Indian suttee, ancient burial rites, and so on: the King lies arrayed on a high pile of wood, ringed by wives and serving girls and soldiers and armor and chattel, the regalia of his eminence. Then the whole is set on fire in an all-consuming blaze. If there is water he sets out to sea, and the boat bearing him away must burn, from keel to topmast: flame. It was the image with which I began and the first scene I wrote.

The manuscripts of my Vermont trilogy (as well as other, early papers) reside now in the Abernethy Room of the Middlebury College Library in Middlebury, Vermont. I have not consulted them. But somewhere in those cartons is the scene of Judah Sherbrooke, lying on a hay bale in the middle of his hay barn in the middle of his property and, by extension, the world. He sets himself afire and, operatically, dies. I wrote and rewrote till it seemed letter-perfect; even today, more than half my life later, I remember the satisfaction of that "pyrotechnical" prose and those funerary rites. The scene was, I was sure, triumphal: a set piece to make Faulkner or Lowry or even James Joyce proud. But I can praise it so unreservedly because it's in an archive and never exposed to the harsh light of print, in the event I cut those pages out.

Judah's elements indeed consist of fire and earth (his young bride's are air and water), and there are leftover traces of the language in Hal Boudreau's drunken fiery accident at the end of *Sherbrookes.* Too, at the end of *Possession,* the old man lies down on his pallet of hay and strikes a match or three. But by the time I'd lived with him and was fully engaged in writing the book, I knew this particular character would not burn down the house. He's too much of a skinflint, too property-proud and retentive to set the world ablaze. Instead, Judah brushes himself off, shambles up and down the street, then back into the kitchen to share a cup of coffee with his wife. It's a much less dramatic—even an anticlimactic—conclusion, but a more truthful one. During the process of composition I had come to understand that, far from destroying himself, this flinty old Vermonter would keep on keeping on.

And that's when I conceived of a second volume and why he does not die. Or, rather, he dies *between* the first two books and not at the end of *Possession,* just as Hattie dies at the end of *Sherbrookes* and Maggie leaves at *Stillness's* end. It's a technical challenge, of sorts; the protagonist of book 1 must be a presence in but not central to the action of book 2; a central character in book 2 is absent from the action of the third installment. In that sense, these three books are not sequels but sequential, and that's when I understood I'd not be finished at *Possession*'s close but needed to resume the story. As Conan Doyle discovered when he tried to kill off Sherlock Holmes and was forced, by an avid public, to bring his hero back to life, it's best—if you do plan to continue—to keep characters alive. In my end was my beginning, therefore; when I scrapped the scene of Judah's death the trilogy proper commenced.

In book 2 the focus shifts, and in book 3 it does so again. A single long novel would perhaps not be built this way, but no single figure here is *Sherbrookes'* sole protagonist; rather, it's a collective and family history with—counting down from Daniel "Peacock" Sherbrooke—five generations in play. It's difficult if not impossible to ask a reader to shift focus and allegiance text by text; the boy who's wholly absent from book 1, for example, is wholly present for book 3—while his father, Judah, who was thoroughly corporeal in the first book is, by the third, a ghost. I tried to justify all this in part because the narrative concerns itself with parents and their children, the presence of the past. And in part by having Ian Sherbrooke—the surviving son of his mother and father's fierce union—write the whole thing down.

The long middle chapter of the middle section of the final book—(which details Ian's romantic history and his attempt to write a play about his parents' intimate wrangle—is my favorite chapter in *Stillness*. (In *Possession* I'm most partial to part II, chapter IV, which begin with the phrase: "Judah met her first, in 1938," and in *Sherbrookes* I like best chapter XIV, describing Maggie's emblematic visions: "Images afflict her; she cannot keep them from coming.") This is, of course, only one man's opinion, but the recapitulatory nature of Ian's rehearsal of what went before does seem to me a successful attempt to lend shape to the whole. It's a tip of the cap, I suppose, to the metafictional and self-reflexive strategies that were so common in the 1970s— an attempt to meld the modern and the more traditional mode.

At any rate, when Ian summarizes his family's history (as well as, it happens, this novelist's previous publications), I knew that the book neared its end. Andrew Kincannon—that outlier—is meant to provide a kind of perspective to the goings-on in the Big House; when he and Maggie and Jane drive off at the end of *Stillness,* the ongoing agon is over and Ian's work truly begins.

*

A thing that surprised me, rereading, is the inadvertent way in which these pages have become "historical." It's strange to see that what one wrote when young is today a period piece and equally strange to read what proved predictive—how these characters' imagined future has since come to pass. There are no cell phones in *Sherbrookes,* and certainly no iPads or computers; when people write to each other they write letters, not email or text messages; when they need to make a call they find a phone. I'm struck, in *Stillness,* by how Andrew Kincannon has to dial the weather number (WE6–1212) in order to get information on the forecast storm, and how he—generously, for the time—hands the garage attendant a dollar. Things change. In these three books, and even when pregnant, everybody drinks and everybody smokes. When Maggie *does* get pregnant at the age of fifty-two, she's a medical anomaly; now that would be a bit less startlingly the case. The Packard Ian drives (and Judah purchased for his wife) is a conscious anachronism; the Plymouth Volare has become one also, but wasn't intended as such. Maggie reminds herself that "these are the facts of inflation, not value," but the price of a stamp or housekeeper's wages or psychoanalytical session has increased exponentially. Her sister-in-law is outraged that soda water costs thirty-five cents a bottle, plus deposit; we'd all be glad of that now.

By contrast, however, most of the geopolitical concerns remain pertinent—or have today surfaced again. *Sherbrookes* spans the years 1976 to 1980, but its characters discuss the price of oil and the possibility of boycotts or an OPEC embargo; they worry about global warming and the infrastructure's collapse. Many of the speeches about the trouble with and in America have, alas, the ring of current truth.

The thematic oppositions of Maggie and Judah—their ways of living in the world—have dulled a little, however, and lost some of their contemporary sheen. The novels deal with the then-much-more-vocal contrarieties of "flower power" and cultural conservatism, the ideals of liberation—particularly, here, in terms of gender—and the straitlaced desire to preserve what went before. I never really saw my heroine as wanton or promiscuous, but it's true that, by the standards of the time and place, she was a kind of revolutionary. Perhaps I should have been explicit about the clash of values and the way this specific family was supposed to embody the general national case; it's not an accident that Judah is seventy-six years old in our bicentennial year. At any rate I took for granted, and possibly more than I should have, the backdrop of the Civil Rights Movement, the emergence of a drug culture, and the generational wrangle which put Ian and Judah at odds.

Other aspects of the story, though I here attempt to retrieve them, have been lost. Those years at Bennington were made vivid for me by the presence of the novelist John Gardner; we were close colleagues and friends. I showed him the manuscript of *Possession,* for example, and we argued over the spelling of Sherbrooke—John insisting that the final "e" was an instance of my Anglicisms and should properly be cut. He came up with a bottle of Sherbrook Whiskey in order to buttress his point; that bottle appears in this book. (The town of Sherbrooke, near Montreal, does have a final "e" attached, and therefore I retained my own preferred orthography.) John, who wrote at warp speed then, preceded me into print with a novel called *October Light,* which won the National Book Critics Circle Award for 1976. In it, he has *his* Vermonters joke about mine; his villagers tell tales about the goings-on in the Big House and mock old Judah Sherbrooke and his "bare-nekkid wife."

My own wife and I make a cameo appearance in the pages of *October Light,* on the dance floor of a local bar. Like many other authors, I had been written about, flatteringly or unflatteringly, as a character before. But to have a creature of my invention be referred to in another's book did seem a kind of testimonial to the power of the written word, and I returned the compliment by having my townspeople in *Sherbrookes* gossip about James Page, Gardner's protagonist, as an "old fool" stuck up in a tree. This cheerful back-and-forth was noticed by a critic in, if I remember correctly, *Newsweek,* who complained about it as a form of literary incest, but the lines still make me smile.

Less happily, I took the title *Stillness*—having asked him for the use of it—from a manuscript of Gardner's he assured me he'd abandoned and was not planning to publish. (Other working titles for the third of my three novels were "Shoreline Certainties" and "Boats in Bottles," both of which appear as phrases and of which John disapproved. He was, I've no doubt, right.) After his death in a motorcycle accident at the age of forty-nine, it devolved upon me as his literary executor to usher into print the unfinished text of *Shadows,* the manuscript on which he had been working when he died. We paired it with his as-yet-unpublished novel, *Stillness,* and there's an echo in these titles—though my own book appeared before Gardner's—which now sounds more mournful than glad.

*

So what, in my seventh decade, would I change and how revise—beyond the ways I've detailed here—these books? The models for my minor figures were sometimes not-so-distantly based on people I knew (Apollonius Banos and Junior Allison were portraits of, respectively, a college friend and a North Bennington taxicab driver), and sometimes an amalgam of townspeople; Elvirah Hayes, Hal Boudreau, and Sally Conover all had their distant counterparts in local village folk. The Old People's Home is an actual structure; the bank and library and grocery store exist. The pavements of North Bennington were marble once; no more. John G. McCullough is long since dead; so is his older sister (who bore scant resemblance to Hattie); the Toy House and the Carriage House and the Big House now operate in fact as a museum and may be rented out for concerts and wedding receptions. When our younger daughter got married, it was in that very house.

In the way most writers, magpie-like, choose to line their nests with scraps of past experience and fragments of encounter, I borrowed attributes of men and women I knew or observed for the central quartet of characters (Judah, Hattie, Maggie, Ian). Yet this is no roman-à-clef or private code to crack. It is an amplification of that begetting image of a funerary pyre and the phrase about King David and Abishag the Shunammite: *but the king knew her not.* The countryside does play, I think, as large a role as I at first envisioned; the trees and stone walls and snow-covered meadows retain a kind of "stillness" on the page.

What emerges for me now, rereading, is how absolute these figures are, how uncompromising in their argument. Judah burns the piano Maggie played on, sells the truck she had incised a heart on in the fender's dust, and never goes to visit when she asks. Jeanne Fisk is much more a relativist, a modern woman, caught between allegiances, who tries to eat her cake and have it too. At its best this book does capture two ways of behaving and—though all this seems clearer to me as reader than decades ago as writer—the clash between the clenched fist and the open hand. The thematic matter of *Sherbrookes* consists, I think, of a young man's puzzled effort to come to terms with commitment: which lines to draw in what sand. It is a book about landscape and the lasting nature of love.

The language of the letter-writers (Peacock, Anne-Maria his daughter, and Judah's father Joseph) looks a little too elaborate today: more representative, I think, of the eighteenth century than the nineteenth. But this I largely left alone, since I hoped for a declension in the generations, and I used their rhetorics to mark the march of time. The language of the Vermonters (paradoxically the more so when they speak at length than when they go "Ayup ayup") is pretty close to the mark. Or at least it feels as near as I could come then and now. I did, I believe, a creditable job of describing Judah and his octogenarian sister, but overstated his sexual appetite and understated, a little, the old man's need for sleep. Maggie's behavior when depressed in *Stillness* feels more persuasive to me than her exuberance in the first two books, but that's no doubt a function of this reader's present age. And the character of Ian—closest, of course, to a self-portrait in these pages—appears to me more successfully composed today than I thought then; his efforts at self-definition seem more a function of personality than a failure of precision on the author's part. He's a beginner, our Ian, who grows up at novel's end.

His creator did so too. Not much happens in these pages: men and women live and die. They grieve and cleave together; they eat and argue and are selfish or selfless and cantankerous or kind. Yet (three decades after finishing the Sherbrookes trilogy) it has pleased me to revisit these old haunts and walk, as it were, those old meadows and trails. And, sentence by paragraph by page, to revel in the view.

Towards an Autobiography

N.B. The Gale Research Company published a series of quasi-scholarly tomes before the Internet came along to make the use of their thick books superfluous. One such encyclopedia was the Contemporary Authors Autobiography Series, and in 1985 I contributed an entry to the second volume. At forty-three years old, I was about to leave Vermont for Michigan and happy to look back. Sandwiched alphabetically in between the poets Cid Corman and Robert Duncan, I wrote ten thousand words of retrospect. Then, fifteen years later, I was asked to supply an appendix and, at fifty-eight, complied. By 2000 the series had reached Volume 189, with the jaw-cracking subtitle of *A Bio-Bibliographical Guide to Current Writers in Fiction, General Nonfiction, Poetry, Journalism, Drama, Motion Pictures, Television, and Other Fields.* As the term *Bio-Bibliographical* suggests, the focus here is on the work of words and "The Writers' Trade."

These two essays have been published but are, to my knowledge, gathering dust in the stacks of research libraries and not part of common parlance or on the everyday shelf. They were handsomely printed and presented; they molder nonetheless. Absent the lavish black-and-white photographs, I reprint them here. It makes for seeming-anachrony, however; in the first installment my father and such friends and teachers as John Updike are alive. As I wrote then, "My elder brother lives in Lexington, Massachusetts" and "my younger brother . . . lives in Watertown." Now they reside, instead, in Cambridge, Massachusetts, and New York, New York. In the second section, I also refer to colleagues in the present tense who, alas, are dead . . .

Time marches on. Now, more than thirty years after that first entry, I want to add a third installment and bring the wheel full circle—though not, I hope, to a full stop. Here, then, are three sequential essays on one writer's life.

*

I was born in London, England, on 27 August 1942. My parents were German Jews who fled, separately, to England; there they were married in 1938. My older brother, Thomas, was born two years to the day before Pearl Harbor. And family legend has it that when Hitler invaded Russia—thus diverting energy from an all-out assault on Great Britain—my mother turned to her husband and said, "He's made a mistake. We may survive. Let's have another child."

So my small history begins with holocaust, and my first roots in the landscape of a London under siege. Tolstoy claimed to remember the womb. I cannot distinguish, however, which memories are actual and what I remember having been told till I nodded in acknowledgment and said, "Yes, yes, that's right." In order of ascending probability, these things: the blackout and air raid the day I was born, the neighbor who brought jam to the house because my mother shouted so in childbirth, the air-raid shelter that had once been a garage. My father painted animals on the rocky protuberances of the wall—so we slept, as a family, under the protective eye of elephants, rabbits, giraffes. I remember loving chocolate in its rationed scarcity; we kept chickens, and once they escaped. My mother's brother arrived from America, bearing a chicken, coffee, and bananas; those were the first bananas I ate. We lived in Hampstead Garden Suburb, a short walk from the heath. I remember hedgehogs in the road, a stand of trees at the crest of our hill that I called Sherwood Forest. We had goose-berry bushes and gooseberry jam. I learned how to whistle before my brother could, and therefore tormented him, whistling.

There was fog so wetly thick at night that our father walked in front of the car, using the beams as a lantern. The house he looked for and we found was brick, with a circular driveway: Number 23, Holne Chase. My mother lost a jewel from a ring in the pebbles of the driveway once, and I spent hours sifting through the pebbles; she had promised a reward. I was known as "Nick the looker"—close to the ground and downward-focused; even today, I spot four-leaf clovers more readily than birds. I had no doubt I'd find the stone and earn the promised pound. My brother did. He saw the head of Minerva in a section I'd not yet scoured, and I was so outraged by the inequity and chanciness of things I set up a howl.

My mother came running. "*I* found it," he said. The ring had value; I too had looked. I got ten shillings as a consolation prize. We were spoiled, of course, and doted on, but this is my first les-son in the way of the world's rewards: cry persuasively enough, and a beneficent committee may give you second prize.

*

Our parents had been raised in affluence. My mother's fam-ily were bankers in Berlin; my father's was in the import-export business in Hamburg. The Delbancos—as the name suggests—had been bankers in Venice: moneylenders originally. One of them, Anselmo Delbanco, had been sufficiently munificent in the sixteenth century to stand as a plausible model for Shylock: a merchant who floated the fleet. In 1630 the Delbancos went to Germany, remaining there three hundred years. And often, in my childhood, I had the sense of diminution: of pictures in muse-ums that had once been in the family, of chauffeurs and upstairs maids and cooks mysteriously seized by Hitler to make us taste poverty's edge.

It's a heightened fantasy: we were never all that rich and never poor. The furniture was hefty, plush, the china and silver intact. A certain smell of polish—a thickness of cigarette smoke in the air, the floors and sideboards thickly waxed, nuts and Sacher torte waiting uncovered—hovers in my nostrils still. The light is bright; my mother disliked candles. The walls are dark with objects, which the maid must dust at peril: African masks, shields, and totems of all sorts; pre-Columbian statuary; graphic work of Goya, Rembrandt, and particularly Lautrec. We called a funerary figure from China "The Chinese Lady"; a demon mask hung in the entrance hall. I used to take comfort in the certainty no robber would be brave enough to pass beneath those protuberant eyes and bristling horsehair beard. There were ceremonial jade blades. I practiced hefting chieftain's spears and glared balefully back at monkey skulls and masks with dried antelope skin. Portraits of my mother as a girl or grandmother in her garden stood kitty-corner to a battle-god, his wooden bulk studded with nails.

I'm told I was a placid child, and plump. My father's mother called me "Buddha," because I sat cross-legged and smiling in the pram; when we first went to the seashore, I said, "My, what a big puddle." I attended Miss Jamaiker's Kindergarten down the road; my brother went to The King Alfred School. I remember sitting on the coal-pile by the chute, or playing "King of the Castle" with Robert Elkeles—he was "the dirty rascal," and I pelted him with coal. We had a red-headed cook called Kathleen who had glass in her thumb; it acted up something awful, she told me, once a month. There was the excitement of tunnels in the tube and an advertisement for Coleman's Mustard ("You must not eat the nation's meat without the nation's mustard") I could spell, then read.

We visited the Isle of Wight, Trafalgar Square, a green frog-fountain in Switzerland where the frog emitted water from its mouth. Our parents spoke German together but were bent on improving their English; my mother was proud of her accentless French. Proud of many things, I think: her taste in shoes and handbags, her childhood friendship with their neighbor Ernst Cassirer, her previous suitors, her sons. Later on, when I grew restive, she would tell me that Manhattan in the liberated sixties was as nothing to Berlin.

Our father cooked kippers with us furtively; his wife despised the smell. On Saturday mornings the three male members of the family would steal to the kitchen together, close the interior doors, and open the out-facing windows. Unwrapping the secretly purchased bundle, our father would turn on the fan and plop fish in the frying pan while my brother and I huddled to the table, sniffing the salty promise, swigging orange juice. We ate like conspirators, quickly. An hour later, with the windows wide open, the fan still on, the lady of the house made her appearance.

"It's horrible in here," she said. "It smells like kippered herring. You ought to be ashamed."

*

Fiction is a web of lies that attempts to entangle a truth. And autobiography may well be the reverse: data tricked up and rearranged to invent a fictive self. Why should I believe Lord Russell's assertion that he can remember what his mother told him in the cradle any more than I disbelieve Proust? We've all had the experience of forgotten history, the reinvented past. Then there's self-engendered history, the slightly tailored tale, the story told so carefully we tell it letter-perfect several times in the same night. The novelist imagines history: his protagonist has a maiden aunt, for instance, and it is her birthday. Therefore we should know where the party takes place, whether she prefers chocolate or carrot cake, whether her rejected suitor still wears argyles after his operation for cataracts last winter, and what the weather is this afternoon of August 23. We can make something out of nothing and add to the world with no fear of subtraction, can feed her hundred birthday guests on air . . .

I remember *himbersaft,* the raspberry syrup my grandmother poured into water and stirred. A mountainous, decisive lady, she took me out on "nature walks"—pointing her carved cane at trees and demanding to know their names. If I got it right ("Monkey-tree, granny, and chestnut, and oak,") I could have *himbersqft* and yogurt and chocolate in her room. Karl Schmidt-Rotluff made her jewelry. She smoked like an ill-pointed chimney, dripping ash; she wore only black or gray. Her English disappeared with time; she died at ninety-six, blind, in my uncle's home. "Send me a postcard," she used to say. "But maybe I won't answer. In the country that I'm going to, they don't deliver mail."

In 1948 we came to the United States to stay. This was in part for business reasons: an import-export firm required an American office. My father's was a family business and he, the younger son, had become titular head. (His elder brother, my uncle, had refused to join. He says he staged a breakdown after a month in commerce—and they soothed him with a painting or two and told him to make his own way. He did; his gallery in London—Roland, Browse & Delbanco—sold excellent art for years.) More important, surely, was my mother's feeling that America would take us in and make us welcome—that we would not combat a hierarchical society as insular as Great Britain's. She was correct. To speak with a German accent—particularly after the Second World War—was to engender suspicion; to be first-generation British was to remain second-class.

On the day of our departure, I hid in Hampstead Heath. I did not know their reasons for leaving and did not want to go. The sorrows of the trip, however, were mitigated by my first pair of long pants—flannels presented at the midpoint of the voyage out. To ensure against the perils of immigration, the family traveled first-class. I remember kindly stewards, steamer rugs, broth, caviar, a Zeppelin that lumbered out to greet us like an airborne whale.

We settled in Larchmont, New York. Our first night in the country we stayed in The Hotel Bevan—a superannuated clap-board structure on the Long Island Sound. During an electri-cal storm, the hotel lights went out. I only imagine the darkness of air raids but do remember this arrival: thunder, the jagged immensity of lightning, black water, the candle on the night-stand by the bed. Looking back, I recognize how fortunate we were—perhaps I knew it even then—to be raised in that place at that time. There was music in the house; my father played the cello, my brother the violin—and I bumped and thumped at the piano, then viola for years. I took painting lessons too, but was thick-fingered, impatient. Hammering, I hit my thumb, sawing, I produced an inadvertent zigzag; when I tried to do the wiring for our electric trains, the transformer shorted out. As a magician—good at patter, I believe, and not bad at card tricks but rotten with scarves—I could never separate the interlinking rings. The elders would sit in their overstuffed chairs, nodding and applauding as I pulled a cotton rabbit from a collapsible silk hat. They drank schnapps and smoked cigars. Now I know that they approved of my showmanship and fervor; then I thought what they applauded was my sleight of fist.

Words were magic from the start: Edward Lear, then Lewis Carroll, Ogden Nash, the lovely lilt of rhyme. I recited things—at birthday dinners, in the bathroom, in the crook of the Japanese maple that flared on the front lawn. I wore a cowboy hat. I had a fringed shirt with mother-of-pearl buttons, a pistol and holster set with rawhide to tie round my leg. I also had a sword. I have not seen it in thirty-five years but would know the feel of it: its wooden handle painted gray, the splintering crosspiece, the light gray blade. One morning in our first October in this country I was playing alone in the yard—waving my sword, shooting my gun, being both Robin Hood and Gene Autry and chasing Indians. I was my own horse also, galloping down the incline to the garden's rear wall. I fell. I landed in a pile of rock where my father left branches to burn. My next memory is of lying in the couch in the sunroom, crying, sucking chocolate; I had broken my left arm. My mother called the doctor and we went to the hospital; soon I was strapped to a cold metal table, and then I had plaster to write on, and a sling.

I was, I suppose, an active child—moderately graceful in sports, happy heaving basketballs or practicing the Statue of Liberty play with my cousin who lived two doors down. We played baseball and tennis, and swam. But at this remove what I remember of my childhood is quiescent; I'm lying in bed with a book. When I was ten I came down with strep throat; it became rheumatic fever, and I was very sick indeed. For weeks I was confined in bed—propped up on pillows, hallucinating, ringing the silver bell by my bedside when I needed orange juice or to be taken to the bathroom (I could not walk unaided) or simply to be certain that the voices drifting up the stairs were familiar, not strange. I listened to the radio, kept score for Yankee games, and tore through Chip Hilton and Hardy Boy books. A love of reading— the habit of it, really—grew ineradicable then. I had a gentle fifth-grade teacher, and she sent my homework home, and get-well cards from class.

I did get better that year, plumping out again and taking penicillin in a raspberry concoction I can still taste, recollecting the chaise longue in the sun, the slow return to school, the birth of my younger brother Andrew, the rearranged house. I paid visits to a specialist in New Rochelle; he pronounced himself content. I can remember the nurse, her bright black wig, the saline solution they put on my arms and legs in order to facilitate the electrocardiogram: yards of patterned signaling from my silent center that they, not I, could scan.

We drove Oldsmobiles, had poodles; we played ping-pong, tennis, chess. I grew embarrassed at my parents' strangeness, the way they failed to understand Mickey Mantle's excellence or Elvis Presley's charm. They talked funny and were formal and would never ever guess that I kissed Carol Weller over popcorn when we triple-dated at *Breaking the Sound Barrier,* or that she said I was cute. I examined myself minutely in the mirror and practiced singing "Oh My Papa," with just the breaking catch in the voice that Eddie Fisher had. Later it was "I Have Dreamed," though I had to sing both parts of the duet, not having a beautiful native to join me at song's close.

We moved into a larger house, brick-faced, slate roofed, at 221 Barnard Road. The wine cellar had pictures of pinups and matchbooks from the various nightclubs the previous owner frequented; I'd hide beneath the Gibson girls and dream. I wanted, of course, to be an actor; actors got the girls. When I played Santa Claus in our sixth-grade production, Carol Weller was Mrs. Santa Claus. The rest of the class were elves and helpers, irrelevant as smoke. We were to kiss at scene's end. My father made me a cotton wool beard, but it got stuck in my mouth. She bent above me, smiling, then put her cheek near mine.

*

One related episode, though the relation may seem distant: I am standing by a swimming pool in Sicily. It is February 1970. Mt. Etna has been busy; for the two weeks of our stay in Taormina, smokeclouds have covered its crest. At night, however, things are otherwise; the flame is visible. It rises and falls continually, a red cone across the valley. I face it, trying to sleep. We have been scouting locations for a film: Siracusa, Agricento, Catania—a long string of "Jolly Hotels," where they illustrate the food they serve in laminated photographs on the elevator walls.

I have been working on a screenplay; my collaborator will direct the movie that we write. It is based, and not all that loosely, on my first book; the money has been raised. Our troupe flies south from Rome. We joke about "a holding pattern over Catania," as the quintessence of caution; things have not been going well. The director has stomach trouble. His remedy appears to be cold white wine and oranges; we have these delivered to the pool. They come in quantity. The financiers are caricature moguls; they want our hero to ride a motorcycle through the Mediterranean surf. They would like a little incest during the credits and a lot of it everywhere else.

It is chilly by the pool. Because we are in Sicily, however, and believe it should be warm, we remove our shirts. Our Italian is not good. The poolside phone keeps ringing, and we take turns taking messages. We tell the desk-clerk that it's only the *scrittore* and *registra* at the pool; he needn't bother with calls, we need to concentrate. We toss an orange back and forth. The director has some skill at juggling; he juggles four at a time. When the phone distracts him, he drops the oranges; they split. He picks up the receiver and, furious, shouts, "There's nobody here. Do you understand me? Nobody!"

I laugh. I tell him about Polyphemus, as if he does not know. Local legend has it that the Cyclops flung a boulder we can see from where we stand; he opens our third bottle and we try again. We need a new concept, he says, an altogether new approach. We play catch with the oranges. He throws a curve; I try a change of pace. He throws a knuckler; I miss. The orange falls into the pool. It floats. A train passes beneath us. We agree that all through Europe the most valuable Riviera frontage belongs to the trains. In America they'd rip up the train-bed and build condominiums; we watch while the cars disappear. I suggest we try for silence in the film; he says these folks are voluble. I want their gestures to be hieratic and their language restrained; we recite the lines with which we've agreed to begin. I feed him a pop fly. His return throw is wild; it also falls into the pool. His stomach feels better, he says, he is feeling no pain. We spend ten minutes earnestly at work; we have Olivettis on loan from the office in Rome.

We take a break. The third orange sinks. We wonder if that's telltale somehow, if we can use it: citrus fruit in water, jostling, tumbling in on a deserted beach because the freighter sank. The sun appears. An immense sense of accomplishment hovers at the shallow end: a feeling of good fellowship, of two heads as better than one. Etna ignites; I could swear it. We empty the remaining oranges into the pool but do not swim. They make the movie. It is atrocious. Too many cooks turn the broth into bilge. The telephone rings ceaselessly. We leave the pool. It stops.

*

My elder brother lives in Lexington, Massachusetts. He is a specialist in primary care who has spent most of his professional life at Harvard, at the Beth Israel Ambulatory Care Center; he is, I am told, first-rate at his work. He has a happy family (marriage to a high-school sweetheart, one son just off to college, two daughters); his garage makes manifest the achieved American dream (a station wagon, a foreign car, lawnmowers, bicycles and skis in size places, camping equipment, maintenance tools, the jumble of prosperity). My younger brother—our parents called him "the American afterthought"—lives in Watertown. He also teaches at Harvard, though his field is American literature; he is a serious scholar, and a close critic indeed. His wife and he have two children. When our father—just turned seventy-five and happily remarried after our mother's death—surveys his three sons, three daughters-in-law, their offspring, he does so with visible pride. We gathered this last weekend for one of those periodic get-togethers that ratify connectives and celebrate the presence of the past. I showed my daughters the white house in Larchmont where I was raised, and that huge hill I tumbled down, breaking my left arm. It has, perhaps, a two-foot pitch; an adult can take it in stride.

The wines were less remarkable than I would have predicted, the crab and shrimp salads less rich. The accents were heavy, as was the cake. Poodles snouted at cherrywood tables; the men wore their jackets in heat. We were giddy, speechifying, boastful—talking politics and travel plans and cars. The elder folk approached my brother with their medical problems, as usual; as usual they said they had heard me on the radio or had read a review and were planning sometime soon to try the book . . .

Barbara Gabriele Delbanco died of a brain tumor in 1974. She was sixty-one. It was, I suppose, a merciful death. She had no symptoms until Thanksgiving and was in the hospital by Christmas; by the start of the New Year she was sent home. There she died in early March; our first daughter, Francesca Barbara, would be born that May. There were flurries of hope like spring snow: perhaps it was a stroke, perhaps it could be treated, perhaps it would remit. But our neighbor, a neurologist, had known from the first night: My mother was alone. She picked up the phone to tell him she was feeling poorly; the receiver fell. Her speech was slurred. Our neighbor called my father—on a business trip in Europe—and told him to fly back.

The cancer proved inoperable. Benign in nothing other than location, the edema acted as its own deadening agent. She needed, at the end, only aspirin. It was a bitter winter: ice storms and a gasoline scare, so that we waited in line to go nowhere, engines spewing cash. We moved into the third floor of the house on Barnard Road. One day my wife and I drove north to check on our own home—abandoned for those weeks, with the kitchen under construction. We arrived to walk through wreckage, turned on the heat and the lights. The phone rang, bringing the news of death.

I learned, I think, proportion. My brother is a doctor, my father well-insured; we all did whatever we could. So the forces of medicine, money, and love were ranged to do battle with something the size of a pea in her brain. It was no contest; the pea won hands down. Unnumbered hours by her bedside notwithstanding, I was not there the day my mother died. The readiness is all. I have written of this obliquely; someday perhaps I will face it head on and at length. The roses on the Meissen and the Rosenthal, the roses on the library table, the horsehair mattress with the ineradicable bloodstains of my brother's birth, the martinis we shared, her love of the mountains, of reading, of chess—the sense I had from first awareness of her imperial adoration and ambition channeled through her sons, so that nothing but the best was good enough, and that only barely, from clothing to girlfriends to grades—the legacy is palpable. I scattered her ashes; that's all. As one of my characters—a sketch for her unfinished portrait—says, "They can't take what you carry in your head."

*

My books were as different, the one from the other, as it lay within my competence to manage. I had and have the notion that the craft of composition is like that of other crafts: we must serve an apprenticeship in order to gain skill. Part of that apprenticeship is involuntary—the reading and writing, the speaking and sedulous aping that mark the age-stages of growth. But because we are born speaking English, read it as soon as we read, write it as soon as we write, we labor under the illusion that we can speak, read, and write. Such familiarity can breed contempt. No one presumes to give a dance recital without having first mastered the rudiments of dance, to perform Mozart before they've learned scales, or to enter a weight-lifting contest if they've never hoisted weights. Yet Here Comes Everybody with their Book of Dreams . . .

I have been the full-fledged student of a writer only once. John Updike is, I think, one of the most literate and able critics of our time. His breadth of reading, acuity of insight, and grace of expression must give most scholars pause; he would no doubt be welcome at any institution in any of the fifty states. But he has remained at a stiff arm's remove from academe and has earned his living by the pen alone. In the summer of 1962, however, his resolution wavered and he agreed to teach—at Harvard Summer School. I wanted to remain in Cambridge and therefore applied for the course. It was an offhand decision; I barely had heard of his name. When he accepted me into his fiction workshop, it would have been ungrateful to drop out.

In retrospect I see more clearly how lucky and right was that choice. The first word I wrote for Updike was the first of my first novel. Like any self-respecting undergraduate, I intended to be either a poet, folksinger, or movie-star. I considered *prose* and *prosaic* to be cognate terms. (They are, admittedly, but I know something more by now about the other three professions and would not trade.) The young man's fancy is poetic, and his models are Rimbaud or Keats. Mine were, at any rate; my first compositions were suicide notes. But I was signed up for a writing workshop with no idea of what to write and not much time to decide. The day of that decision is vivid to me still.

A friend and I were strolling around a lake in Wellesley; we'd been reading for final exams. I heard him out as to his future; then he had to listen to me. I had tried my hand already at the shorter stuff, I said; I was going to write a novel. That was what a summer should consist of—something ambitious, no piddling little enterprise like Chekhov's but something on the scale of, let's say, *Moby Dick*. Yet before I wrote my masterpiece I had to plan it out. What do first novels consist of, I asked—then answered, nodding sagely at a red-haired girl in a bikini emerging from the lake. First novels are either the myth of Narcissus or the parable of the Prodigal Son, but generally disguised. Their authors do not understand they fit an ancient mold. I already knew enough about Narcissus, I confessed, and therefore would elect the latter; I'd rewrite the parable. The difference was that my revision would be conscious—whereas most young novelists fail to see themselves in sufficiently explicit mythic terms.

That was not my problem, but there were problems to solve. I knew nothing about the landscape of the Bible, for instance, and should find a substitute. My friend lit a cigarette; we considered. It happened that I'd been to Greece the previous summer and traveled wide-eyed for weeks. I would replace one location with the other. The parable has three component parts: the son leaves home, spends time away, and returns. My novel too would have three components, with Rhodes and Athens as its locales. My Greek protagonist would go from the island to city and "eat up his substance with whores."

The girl in the bikini trailed drops of water where she walked; she shook her long hair free. I instructed my friend that *hetaerae* in Athens had "Follow Me" incised backwards on their sandals, so they could print directions in the dust. She rounded a bend in the path. The question of contemporaneity engaged me for three minutes. I knew enough about modern-day Greece to fake it, possibly, but knew I'd never know enough about the ways of antique Attica; the prostitute's sandal exhausted my lore. It would take less research to update the parable. So there, within ten minutes, I had it: a contemporary version of the parable of the Prodi-

gal Son that followed the text faithfully and yet took place in
Greece. The rest was an issue of filling in blanks; I started to,
next week.

I have told this tongue-in-cheek, but it is nonetheless true.
The epigraph of *The Martlet's Tale* is the first line of the parable;
the great original is buried in my version, phrase by phrase. I
revised the novel many times and by the time I'd finished was no
longer a beginner. Looking back I'm astonished, however; it all
fell so neatly in place. The editor at Lippincott ushered me into
his office and agreed to bring out the book. "You're a very fortunate young man," he said, but I thought his politeness routine. I
took success for granted when it came. My photograph in maga-
zines seemed merely an occasion for judging the likeness; a long
and flattering review in the *New York Times* on publication day
was no more than an author expected; I ate expensive lunches
with the cheerful certainty that someone else would pay.

In some degree, moreover, this very blindness worked to my
advantage. I had been accustomed to a schoolboy's notion of success. I would have dealt with failure far less equably. Had Updike
not encouraged me, I cannot say for certain if I would have persevered; there were many wind-scraps in the wind, and I followed
the favoring breeze. Harvard does prepare you for the world in
this one crucial way: if you succeed within its walls, you assume
that you will when outside. When I handed in *The Martlet's Tale's*
first chapter, and my professor's reaction was praise, I concluded
that the rest must follow as the night does day. I suppose I stood
out in his class; I certainly tried to; his wary approval meant
much. I wrote a second chapter and was hooked.

Briefly, then, these followed: *Grasse 3/23/66* and *Consider Sappho Burning.* Those two books were largely formal experiments:
the first an "orphic mystery," the second a parable of the five
senses, narrated by the sixth. Then I wrote a more public novel,
News, though this too was organized by a formal model—that
of the synoptic gospels. *In the Middle Distance,* my fifth book,
is a fictive autobiography, and *Fathering* a truncate version of
the Theban trilogy. *Small Rain,* the seventh novel, appeared

nine years after the first; it took its shape and story from that of Tristan and Isolde. J. B. Lippincott and Company published the first two books, and William Morrow and Company has been my publisher since. Jim Landis of the latter firm bought *Consider Sappho Burning* and *News,* and then we were paired. I could not ask for a better or more devoted friend.

The three novels of the Sherbrookes trilogy (*Possession, Sherbrookes,* and *Stillness*) seem to me to have marked the transition from apprentice to journeyman laborer. These books are neither built around a previous structure nor modeled consciously on the work of others; they take place where I've come to call home. My first novel's locale was Greece, my seventh the south of France; in between I'd ranged as freely as my passport permitted—writing of that rootlessness that seeks to ratify roots. I have lived in Vermont, however, since 1966. And though that makes me no sort of native it does permit a kind of focus—a deepening, perhaps. I do not propose here to write at length of my own writing; that seems to me more properly the task of others. By 1980, however, I had accumulated novels and nearly nothing else.

Friends urged me to try my hand elsewhere, to work in different genres and at a different pace. That seemed sensible. I had no further need or desire to write a novel a year. And I have made my living as a teacher, discussing other authors—their variety and range. So it was a welcome change to write *Group Portrait: Conrad, Crane, Ford, James, & Wells.* I wrote of the community on the border of East Sussex and Kent with the wishful assumption it might prove possible again. Short stories, too, were a departure; the collection *About My Table* takes as its topic the domestic life. I wrote those stories while researching *Group Portrait* and, more recently, *The Beaux Arts Trio.*

*

The only way to learn one's art—a craftsman's paradox—is through backbreaking labor which must not seem like work. Like the dubber in a foreign-language film who most succeeds when no one knows he's around. Or like those Zen masters of the martial arts. After the body has been trained to achievement, trained so that what earlier seemed impossible is difficult, difficult habitual, and the habitual easy—at the point where everything is instinct, true mastery begins. The highest *dan* cannot be attained; the highest attainable dan is reached through meditation. So we have the spectacle of the ancient jiu-jitsu *sensei,* crumbled into the carapace of age, sitting on his tatami mat in the sun. And a disciple—full of health and radiant muscularity—comes up and assumes an attack stance and says, "Master, I must kill you now," and raises the axe. But the sensei pulls out the rug from under his student's feet.

I have urged myself to practice, trusting to the notion of perfection later on. We are all of us apprenticed to a fast-vanishing guild; the species is endangered and much mastery is specious nowadays. Hunt that old codger in the sun, I tell myself, but don't swing your axe if you find him. Look up his sleeves with reverence, and keep at a respectful distance from the mat.

It's fun, of course, such babble; we ought admit to that. If there weren't pure pleasure in the way words edge up against each other, in the way paragraphs fit, in learning how catachresis can prove serviceable—then we'd all have to be a higher- and bloodier-minded bunch. Because the average wage is maybe a penny a page, or dime each twenty hours; the average reward is anonymity. If your name is well enough known to be taken, then it's likely to be so in vain, or *mispelled*; vanity and sottishness and the deep paralysis of repetition await those who truly succeed. We dream of influence; it's effluence instead. Those who hunt success too consciously are conscious of too little else; those to whom it comes unbidden do its bidding soon. It's easy to inveigh against the writer's rotten lot, to say we're blessed or cursed or necessary prophets without honor and too few who're honorably with. But there are other professions, and most professional wordsmiths could find some other job. They don't; they won't; why not? One answer is, it's fun.

*

We string a set of moments into continuity. It is the last day of June. One morning—this one—may stand as an emblem for most. There was a fierce thunderstorm last night, and it woke the children. The grass is wet. I rose at six, let the dog out and the cat in, made coffee; Elena, my wife, left at seven to shop. On this final Saturday of the month, the supermarkets will be full by nine and unmanageable at noon; she needs to provision us early. The Bennington Writing Workshops begins; our friends—the faculty—arrive. We shall feed twenty or so for dinner. In the month to come our house will be invaded, and it is a welcome but high-pitched invasion: writers from all over the country, bands of children, continual shoptalk and gin. Mary Robison drove here from Ohio, George Garrett from Maine, Dave Smith from Richmond, Virginia; Carolyn Kizer arrived by plane from California, Richard Elman drove north from New York, Jon Manchip White and Alan Cheuse from Knoxville, Tennessee

The Green Mountains beyond the meadow—it needs cutting; a red-wing blackbird flutters past—look blue-gray in the haze. The mosquitoes are fierce. Our vast puppy, Major Scobie, cracked a flowerpot. The children stir. Francesca, ten, and Andrea, six, have a visitor—a girl whose mother died recently and who has been spending the week. I read them to sleep in the bunk-room with the Bernard Miles version of *Romeo and Juliet*; they preferred the previous text, *Twelfth Night*.

Yesterday I had a conversation with a friend from half my life ago who has been away for years. He has been living in France. He spent eighty-five days on a solo sail to Easter Island; he was rescued by a freighter when he thought he'd surely die. The last fifteen days before sighting he had been on his knees, in near-paralysis; the wife of the radio operator happened to notice his flare. This puts matters in perspective. He praises—with the slightly mocking envy that has structured our association—my garden, my mannerly children, books, this vista, my beautiful wife. He tells me that I try too hard for order, that I should use a pseudonym and let the outlaw out. I thin the radishes. He has a point. But the work, I tell him, how could I get up each winter morning and get down to work if the woodstove's not stoked, the wood stacked?

Where I sit, at the edge of the lawn, I have been sitting for years. There are no houses visible. Our own is a remodeled barn. I play solitaire to keep still at the keyboard: a Hermes 3000 portable which, when the weather lifted, I have hauled outside. Elena returns, unpacks the groceries, starts frosting the cakes she produced at midnight; the phone rings often. It's a busy imitation of silence; the radio offers Franz Schubert's "The Trout." Andrea will wake cranky till she has a bowl of Froot-Loops and turns on the TV; this is "cartoon morning," and she loves the Smurfs. I should weed the lettuce and read a manuscript forwarded by one of the workshop students—an avid lady who has sent four hundred pages in advance. Of the seven games of solitaire since starting on this sequence, I have won one, been blanked once, and done respectably on two. The white siding of the house steams in the increasing heat; the split-leaf maples drip.

*

I went to the Fieldston School, and then to Harvard College. At the time I was convinced, of course, my personality and problems were extraordinary; now they seem representative. And in this finite space I'll curtail that time—as well as, later, the years spent at Columbia University. I received a BA from Harvard and was graduated magna cum laude; my thesis had the improbable topic "A Comparison of the *Neue Gedichte* of Rainer Maria Rilke and *Les Trophées* of Jose Maria de Heredia," with particular reference to two poems on the birth of Aphrodite. At Columbia I was a Woodrow Wilson Fellow, an International Fellow, and an Edward John Noble Leadership Fellow, studying International Relations; for a brief period I dreamed of work in that world. My master's thesis was in English and Comparative Literature; I wrote of Malcolm Lowry's *Under the Volcano*.

There are memories that now seem emblematic of those years: the tennis courts in late afternoon light, the Seventy-Ninth Street underpass off the West Side Highway, and my furtive jostling of that week's companion as we turned, family trips to Europe, driving lessons, my first car. I tried to sing, tried to play the guitar. I grew my hair as long as my parents would permit, fancied myself an actor and, later, a director. There's the look of Cambridge in the rain, the taste of an Elsie's Special, heavy on the dressing, the sound of Leon Bibb and Joan Baez and Bob Dylan and Odetta, the feel of Harris tweed and flexed pectoral muscles and, astonishingly, female flesh. That was the true study of those years. For every memory I have of Anglo-Saxon verb forms, I can remember ten times over the smile of the blonde to my right. It's a common story, also, and can be summarized: my dreams of conquest were of women, and of battlefields the bed.

In the summer of 1960, I stumbled on "true love." The term is coy, requiring quotes, but it remains authentic from this adult vantage; Carly Simon was my pearl among white peas. I was seventeen, she sixteen; we were wide-eyed children who clung to each other for years. She introduced me to her family, to Martha's Vineyard—an island I called, happily, home—and to requited lust. She is the dedicatee of my first book, the cover girl and subject of my second. After college I returned to London, to work in my uncle's art gallery; neither the place nor the profession took. Carly joined me, and we settled in the south of France, but the reality of housekeeping soon drove us apart. We were not ready for marriage, and it would have been the logical next step. She grew increasingly public and I grew increasingly jealous—not of her fame, I think, but her indiscriminate-seeming sweetness. There was much bitter wrangling over who betrayed whom how. But I have never lost and want to record here the sense of great good fortune in that early choice; we were kind to each other, more often than not, and watched the world unfolding like a map of trips to take.

I came to Bennington, Vermont, in 1966. Bernard Malamud was leaving the small college for a year in Cambridge; he would need to be replaced. My first book was not as yet published, and I had never taught but nonetheless applied. I heard nothing for some months—had only half-expected to—and was not surprised. Then one day in a snowstorm I found myself near Bennington, returning to Manhattan from a ski trip to Stowe. I called the critic Stanley Edgar Hyman—the department "secretary"—who told me to drop by. I did; we had a drink; members of the Language and Literature Division appeared. The snowstorm had been fierce. We chatted with what seemed to me casual inconsequence; I continued south with the sense that it had been a pleasant visit, nothing serious. They offered me the job. I accepted and stayed on.

We rarely know when crossing it that we have crossed a divide; a turning point grows visible once passed. In retrospect I understand how crucial was that interview. I owe much to this college and will not leave it lightly—though I've taught, in the past years, at Skidmore, Trinity, and Williams colleges, at Columbia and Iowa universities also; it has been the locus of my adult life. I got the notion that resulted in *In the Middle Distance* from a course in "Autobiography," for *Group Portrait* from a course I taught called "Exile"; the action of the Sherbrookes trilogy takes place down the road. I began the Bennington Writing Workshops, together with John Gardner, in 1977.

Yet comfort-rounds of habit begin to seem like limitation; the sense of discovery wanes. Perhaps these crossroads are continual; perhaps we notice the fork and alternative only while we pause. This essay is just such a pause, a chance to assess direction. As of September 1985, we will settle in Ann Arbor—where I will join the English department of the University of Michigan and direct the Master of Fine Arts in Writing. As much my father's junior as my children's senior, I feel Janus-faced these mornings—looking at the distance traveled and the road ahead. One profit of a life in prose is that it fixes mutability—permits one to print, as if constant, a constantly changing intention. We know something of our origin and nothing of our end.

*

Max Eastman was in his eighties when I was in my twenties. We met on Martha's Vineyard and grew close. He welcomed me, whether in Gay Head, New York, or Barbados; he was tolerance incarnate, with an amused abiding sense of how youth preens. I postured; I was working on a book (*Grasse 3/21/66*) that was recondite in the extreme. I'd labor in an ecstasy of self-congratulation, producing perhaps a hundred words a day, intoning the sibilant syllables till they appeared to make sense. One such passage, I remember, contained a quotation from Villon, a description of Hopi burial rites, an anagram of the name of my fifth-grade teacher, an irrefutable refutation of Kant, glancing reference to Paracelsus, suggestive ditto to my agent's raven-haired assistant, paraphrase of Cymbeline's dirge, and an analysis of the orthographic and conceptual disjunction between Pope and Poe. I took my time; I let it extend to ten lines. That night I brought my morning's triumph to Max and permitted him to read. He did so in silence. He tried it aloud; so did I. When he said it made no sense and I explained the sense it made, he looked at me with generous exasperation. "Sure," he said. "That's interesting. Why don't you write it down?"

Like many others, I suppose, I live with a twinned notion of the self. The first: I was a startling, prodigious child who has been declining steadily and will, at sixty, be worthless. The second: I was a boastful egotist who has been gaining in the attributes of manhood and who may amount to something by the age of sixty. Truth resides between. What we lose in energy we hope to replenish by wisdom; what I've lost in daring I'd like to think of as a kind of power-in-reserve. The best work waits ahead. How fearful to think the reverse!—and at this more than midpoint of my actuarial life I sense the first faint stirrings of that fear. But I asked a friend at lunch today—Jon Manchip White, who has just turned sixty—how he feels about his "man-of-letters" career. His wizard's face crackled with glee. "I've had a marvelous time," he said. "I've traveled, been much loved. And when I think of schoolmates, how many of them died in the war, I think of every day as one more gift. Oh yes"—he smiled, he wiped his lips—"I'd do it all over again."

On 12 September 1970, I married the former Elena Carter Greenhouse. We were married in Vermont; we had known each other for years. We met in 1961, while undergraduates, then went our separate crisscrossing ways. Elena is the daughter of the cellist Bernard Greenhouse and Aurora de la Luz Fernandez y Menendez; her grandparents came from Vienna, Riga, and Asturias. She is dark and lush and mercurial and tough. I do not have as yet—nor will I try to acquire—sufficient distance from the marriage to assess it for these pages; it seems to me a strong one, and likely to endure. I love my wife and admire her various competencies, her quicksilver sweetness and noticing eye. She worked in concert management, then with a drug rehabilitation program, then as a psychologist in Bennington; her values are more firm than mine, her sympathies wide-ranging and intelligence acute.

We left the country after our wedding and flew to Sweden, then drove south. I had never been to Germany and did not much want to go. But we stayed the night in Hamburg, in a reconverted private home on the BlumenStrasse; I inquired of the hotelkeeper if she knew where 54, AgnesStrasse—my father's home address—would be. The streets were alphabetically named in that section of the city; she pointed across the canal. Later, in Berlin, at the Branitzer Platz, I located my mother's home—imposing edifices both, the thick stone structures of their childhood given bodily dimension. Elena and I traveled on. We went many places that year it would not now be simple to revisit: Iran, Afghanistan, for instance, and landscapes of romance: a hut on the South Java Sea, a camp in Kathmandu.

Of late our life is located, and we travel when we can. It's a rushed tranquility, a hurried standing still. Friends die, divorce, remarry, retire, make headlines, quarrel, get fat. The children grow. As one of three sons I find it a daily instruction to be the father of daughters instead. Cesca is meditative, inward—a literate person with poise. She has humor and self-assurance

and wants to be an actress; next year she'll no doubt be playing Mrs. Santa Claus. Andrea had a dislocated hip at birth and
spent months in a remedial brace, then a cast. Released, she has
rocketed everywhere—a passionate, spark-sending imp. I work at
home and am distracted often, am often forgetful, abrupt. But
I want to take advantage of this moment, these crossroads, the
page—want to write what they anyhow know. Their parents love
them very much. They are luminous presences, each.

*

A general drift of the novel in our time has been towards self-
consciousness. By "our time" I mean this century; by "self-consciousness" I mean the instructed awareness of tradition, and
one's relation thereto. As genre the novel is relatively new, its
conventions recent. When Cervantes or Fielding or Stendhal sat
down to tell a story, they could do so unimpeded—compara-
tively speaking—by a sense of how their predecessors worked.
The wide world furnished topics, and they might range freely. No
writer of the nineteenth century would hesitate for long before
he made his hero a lawyer, a doctor, an explorer, soldier, scientist,
or cleric; to do so nowadays gives many a novelist pause.

This is in part a function of research. The language of doctors
and lawyers sounds more specialized to our ears than it did to
George Eliot's; the data we require for a convincing portrait of an
atomic physicist might even have halted Balzac. The princes and
captains of whom Murasaki or Conrad could speak have become
the property of the mass-market author and therefore doubly
damned. One signal of the way our age has increased in specialization is the self-reflexive novel; in theory as in practice now we
tend to offer primacy to the world within the word.

There is a concomitant emphasis on form. Few present writers worth their salt would consider a first page finished till they
had composed their last. Pattern (the circle, the parenthesis, the
narrative stance) enters in. The dictates of revision and the vir-

tues inhering in arrangement have been unquestioned lately: self-consciousness values its shape.

So the young man and woman of sensibility take stage center in our books. Often they are sickly or of independent means; often, in pursuit of some spiritual imperative, they hold no daily job. And when they work it's likely to be at the artist's trade. This is a rule to which there are salient exceptions, but it nonetheless applies: more books have been produced of late with the novelist as hero than ever before. Of what else may the writer write authoritatively; what other way of working may we comprehend?

The academy has something to do with this also. Haven and employer for the novelist, it provides a friendly soil for academic texts. The teacher finds it easier—it has proved so for me, at least—to speak of "complicated" books than simple ones, to treat them as ciphers to crack. "Let's see where the Kabbalah enters in; let's discuss the recurrence of the teacup-motif; let's find the Jungian archetype in this subordinate clause . . ." Add the pleasure of puzzle-solving to the *frisson* of the confessional, and you have complicated books about the bookish life. Characters deal with each other as characters; dialogue contrives to be both eloquent and arch; the artifact itself becomes of consequence—a mirror held to nature's mirror, taking pride of place.

*

Some years ago I had a conversation that I carry with me, still, as a cautionary tale. I stopped a farmer—call him Everett Saunders—on his tractor in the road. The lane was little traveled, dirt, and dusty; it was July. He had been commended to me as a man who would sell wood, mow fields, do neighborly labor for a fair price. I had more land than I could handle and was in any case incompetent at farming; I needed help. Everett recognized me also; in that village, any stranger was discussed. "You're the one they call Nick," he said, and killed the motor and lit up his pipe. Puffing, he kept silent while I blundered on about which cows

I'd pasture in which field, what kind of grass I planned to plant and how much he could cut. When I said I was a college teacher and therefore—transparent excuse!—couldn't farm full time, he perked up. He had seven children; one of them was soon to enter nursing school. We had a long discussion, and he took eager part in it: the benefits of education, the value of a degree, the methodology of teaching, the particular instruction that his daughter would receive, the scholarship money available, the high cost of tuition, the risk and yield and loss. He was behind her, Everett said, behind her all the way . . .

Emboldened by such newfound friendship, I offered a personal truth. "I'm a college teacher," I announced, "but that's not all I do. What I really love is writing, I'm a writer, I write books."

His eyes glazed. "Books," he said. He knocked his pipe-bowl empty on the steering wheel. "Don't mean nothing to me." He started the tractor and left. For the five years that I worked at my three novels of the farmer's life—the Sherbrookes trilogy—I tried to remember his answer, that lack of interest and cap-tipping scorn. "Don't mean nothing," say our characters, "to me."

*

The risk of forcing one's voice equals the risk of repetition; ventriloquism proves as wearing as the monotone. The spectacle of academics trying to write like Mickey Spillane is no more edifying than would be the reverse. The writer who keeps shifting ground finds no securer purchase than the one who does not move.

Each novelist, I think, must at some time be seized by a perception of the foolishness, not to say futility, of the enterprise: a grown person making up stories to gain other grownups' attention. We scuttle, pen in hand, to baseball games or bars and come back with our fragment of overheard speech. We rise from our loved one's bed or hospital bedside and make notes; we enter delivery rooms or funeral parlors with the at least partly conscious intention of returning with a phrase. It's a strange profession and affords strange comfort: word-spinning, ghost-spelling, the King sung to sleep. That commonplace injunction to the apprentice author, "Write about what you know," begs the question utterly: we discover what we know while writing, and it is more than we knew.

I have recently completed a book on the Beaux Arts Trio. A nonfiction study of chamber musicians, it presented a problem of voice. I added and invented nothing but translated much. The three artists (Isidore Cohen, violin; Bernard Greenhouse, cello; and Menahem Pressler, piano) are more expressive in music than speech. They avoid the terminology of music criticism; they demonstrate a phrase by singing or playing, not articulating it. Greenhouse is by nature reticent, and Pressler, although voluble, not native to English. The injunction "speak in tongues" became a comic babble when I transcribed tapes. I spent a week with them at La Chaux-de-Fonds—a small town in Switzerland where they record for Philips Records. In conjunction with the Italian violist, Bruno Giuranna, the members of the trio recorded the two Mozart piano quartets. The engineers were Dutch, the piano tuner German. As Giuranna observed, "When musicians must discuss a piece, it's a very bad sign. You must have it in your head, of course, but play it with your heart."

Here is a verbatim rendering of discourse, from my notes and tapes. They were in rehearsal; I will not try to indicate who was speaking when. "*Nun,* take it from D. Wubba wubba wubba wubba. *Ich habe quasi improvisatore ici.* You follow my bowing and I follow yours. Wubba wubba. You lose the whole effect of that *piano* after playing *forte* for fourteen bars through. Last night I tried going up, today I go down—the take-over shouldn't sound as if now it's me—but lead up, please. I'd like a little less activity on that boobooboo-boo. Would it be too Beethoveny if you played it bumbum bum; is there a wedge on each note? No, it's the bush that burns underneath.

"It's *nicht gut.* It's march music. Where do you put the down-beat? Then be careful of the A-flat. The first five notes after the slurred note, could you start a little lighter? That sounds *ver-*

misscht. Did you hit the low E-flat? I'm playing it; fantastic, at the end, how he takes away the chord and leaves the E-flat clear for the piano. Let's try it once just as written, *nun,* from D."

Rounded off, there were fifty hours of such talk for the one completed hour of performance. The recording is, I believe, eloquent, the language clearly not. Or, more precisely, my role was to evoke the nature of the enterprise in a language faithful to but sufficiently distinct from the original to be more than mere transcription. This was a particular problem of reportage and, perhaps, extreme. But it seems to me an emblem of the novelist's ongoing task: we witness and translate.

What we choose to witness is, of course, of consequence: the sounds of a three-fingered amateur ukulele player would be less rewarding to study than those of the Beaux Arts Trio. The death of Anna Karenina has more enduring resonance than does the death of a flea. Yet Tolstoy's transcendent novel took flight from a newspaper story; James built elaborate fictions from the chance dinner-party remark. It is seldom possible to gauge beforehand what will prove a fruitful topic, which anecdote will fire the imagination; some matters move us, some do not. The writer gleans windscraps; he listens whenever he can. Each day is full of instances; what counts, as with all stimuli, is the sympathetic response.

This is not to say the writer need do research of the spirit or back-breaking kind. It should not be forced. Nonfiction and the compendious mass-market saga rely on data principally; fact-checking is but one component of the artist's work. There are better roadmaps to Dublin than Joyce's *Ulysses,* and we would believe the snowstorm in "The Dead" if it had not snowed that day. But if a character is a carpenter, his author has to know the difference between a jig and a handsaw; if the heroine is an Avon lady, we should know what products she sells. When we use up our store of available data—the stuff of childhood, then youth— the professional writer is left with one profession to describe. Then it grows imperative (or every book will be about its own construction) for us to practice "reach."

My argument therefore resolves into this: when the self-conscious author casts about for subject matter, he should pay attention to the visible, audible world. Inflection is as various as fingerprints. We should train our ears and accents as do actors if we hope to play more than one part. The intonation of "self-conscious," for example, has grown pejorative—but few would feel the same of the Greek injunction "Know thyself." Self-consciousness is necessary; it is not sufficient. The voice of the accomplished author will be a chorale.

Autobiography: Addendum
(August 2000)

"The voice of the accomplished author will be a chorale." It's fully fifteen years since I wrote that final line of that previous installment and first pass at remembrance. I was attempting to describe the variety of verbal arrangements and, in a portrait of chamber musicians, the aural issue of tone. This descriptive assertion was also prescriptive, a way of urging myself to use more than one voice in the effort—as William Butler Yeats expressed it lastingly—"to articulate sweet sounds together." In "Sailing to Byzantium" he called it "singing school."

Yeats is one of our culture's great poets, of course, and daunting enough to keep me from trying my own hand at verse. These years I've worked in other modes: book reviews, articles, essays, a travel book, short stories, novels, a play. "Inflection is as various as fingerprints," I wrote—and meant it then, mean it today. Whatever else has been "accomplished," and though it may not "be a chorale," there's new language on the shelf.

Too, I've been struck, rereading, by how much remains the case, how little has been altered even in its outer aspect and how gracious has been the so-far-so-good holding action and benign neglect of time. This is, as they say, life's prime. I write once again from the house in Vermont in the postdawn rising light and staring at the mountains; my wife and two daughters are sleeping upstairs; hot coffee cools in its mug. The dog is dead, alas; the cat survives. My beloved Major Scobie—that vast puppy by my side in 1985—died soundlessly in his twelfth year; Midnight is in her twenties now, and still on the *qui vive* for mice. The meadow, warming, steams.

In the middle distance I hear traffic, but all I can see are the flowers and trees, the wide expanse of lawn. There's the first chill hint of autumn in the morning air, the first leaves dropping from the birch and a flaring tinge of scarlet in the maple at field's edge. My fifty-eighth birthday takes place in a week, my thirtieth wedding anniversary next month, and in some days we'll drive to the town of Ann Arbor, where we work and vote. At the end of that previous entry I had accepted a new job; now we call Michigan home. By "we" I mean my wife and I, my beloved, beautiful Elena: daily and yearly a gift. All praise to her then; all praise now.

My next book—a novel—appears in November; my next work of nonfiction next year. My father, in his nineties, thrives; my two brothers and their families prosper; so does the MFA program in Creative Writing for which I serve as director. I can't pretend, when looking in the mirror or standing on the scale, that everything is as it once was—but there've been no major upheavals or catastrophic shifts. So what follows will be more a postscript and addendum than new chapter, and for this I'm grateful: a constancy in change. What I hoped for in 1985 and hope for in 2000 is, simply, more of the same.

*

Our elder daughter, Francesca, was graduated from Harvard College, then went abroad for a year on a Rotary Fellowship, then moved to New York and is now in Ann Arbor again. In 1985, I called her "a literate person, with poise." That description has held true; she serves as a kind of "Dear Abby" for millions of teenage readers of *Seventeen.* Francesca writes a monthly advice column called "Hard Questions" and is at work on a novel, having earned her MFA in prose fiction last year.

Andrea too writes a column, though weekly—called "Playing in the Neighborhood"—and for the *New York Times*. After receiving her BA from Brown University she moved directly to Manhattan, and our "passionate, spark-sending imp" now describes herself as the one member of the family who holds a steady job. She and her sister are close. At twenty-six and twenty-two they are remarkable young women, both: quick-witted, unpretentious, accomplished, lovely to look at, and *fun*.

These days in Bennington in the house where they were raised have felt like a kind of reunion: walking the familiar trails and driving the familiar roads and eating in the old familiar restaurants and visiting with friends. It's summer's end, the start of a new season and return to school. Elena teaches in the newly named Gerald R. Ford School of Public Policy at the University of Michigan; I direct the Hopwood Awards Program and the MFA in the English department. So Andrea can say, with some justification, that the time clocks we punch are irregular if not slugabed; all academics live the life of Riley, she complains . . .

What follows is an extract from an essay I published two years ago called—once more with a cap-tip to Yeats—"A Prayer for the Daughters." It too remains the case:

> So, yes, I am conditioned by tradition . . . Yes I want my daughters to walk at some point down some aisle on my arm—though I don't require them to wear white or be married in a building that has aisles. Yes I want them to be happy in the way their parents have been, and to emulate as women that exemplary woman who nurtured them throughout their youth and continues to do so today. I recognize that married love is neither original nor, perhaps, now fashionable—but it has made their father happy for nearly thirty years. And what I hope for them is not something other or in contrariety but, also, more of the same.
>
> These verbs *want* and *hope* are not, I trust, imperatives; neither, come to that, is the verb *trust*. Deploy them here as nouns instead, as the conditions of trust and hope and the explicit parental desire to keep children free from want. I would feel the

same way about sons if we had had them, would treat them the same way—both in terms of expectation and the assessment of what's been achieved. But this is moot; I cannot tell; I can only report on the actual . . .

For years we were inseparable as a quartet, going everywhere together and sharing one roof. Now time and the river have done their slow work, and we're together only rarely and on prearranged occasions. This is as it should be. But always still, as soon as possible—and it delights their parents always—the two of them go off together and, from behind their shared closed door, the sound of laughter comes . . .

What I pray now for my daughters is that they have children whose father will admire them as much as I do mine. And what I pray for those children is that their mothers prove as splendid a mother as is and has been their own. I want them safe. I want them healthy, not ill or at risk. I want them protected from want. I mean them to know what they mean.

*

Vladimir Nabokov called his autobiography *Conclusive Evidence,* then revised it as *Speak, Memory.* That second title too had been subject to revision; "Speak, Mnemosyne" was what he planned to call it, in honor of the goddess of remembrance. (Unsurprisingly, his publishers demurred.) Though the sum and substance of my prayer is that things remain the same, time's wheel nonetheless must continue to turn. And since ten thousand words sufficed for my first forty-three years and the first installment, here are a few thousand more.

The dead have added to their lists, of course; Stephen Becker, Richard Elman—to name two of the writers in this series in whose recollections my own name appears—have died in the past fifteen years. When I think of those who hired me at Bennington in 1966—Stanley Edgar Hyman and Howard Nemerov and Bernard Malamud—I think of what James Baldwin (another of my teaching colleagues, though not in the context of college) called "the royal fellowship of death." We are in thrall to time. They all were friends; they all are gone, and now what quickens memory is a few photos on the shelves and their enduring texts . . .

When I took that job at Bennington I did not, could not, know how crucial a decision I was making. In retrospect it's clear to me that all the roads not taken branched off from this particular track and that I've lived my professional life as a teacher of writing. I did not then imagine I would. Nearly thirty-five years later I can recall with clarity my first arrival at the school, my assumption I'd be there a year—maybe two—and move on. Robert Frost lived down the road in Shaftsbury and lies buried in the churchyard in Old Bennington; I'm now the Robert Frost Collegiate Professor at the University of Michigan (where from 1921 to 1923 he was Poet-in-Residence and Fellow in Creative Arts.) In my study in Ann Arbor I have a desk from his house. Whether I chose or was in some sense chosen, whether that choice was casual or causal, the job of teaching is the one I've held and will hold for the entirety of my working life.

The pairing just now of "chose" and "chosen," "held and hold," the anagrammatic juxtaposition of "casual" and "causal"—all these bespeak a consciousness of language and a self-consciousness about it, the way a sailor's walk or mechanic's oil-smudged fingernails can signify their trade. When I tally the sum of "thirty-five years" I think of Dante's age in "the middle of the road of our life"; when I use the word "tally" I think of Walt Whitman as well as tally sheet. I'm hopelessly, in short, a professor, and reading and writing are what I profess . . .

So by now it's only natural that much of my time be spent in the presence of—or, when absent, in appreciative contact with—young writers with whom I have worked. In just this year, for instance, books have appeared by Alyson Hagy, Miles Harvey, Kimberly Kafka, Laura Kasischke, Michael Paterniti, Elwood Reid, Paisley Rekdal, Maxine Rodberg, Porter Shreve, Leah Stewart, and Simone Zelitch of the MFA Program at Michigan; the year before saw books from Michael Byers and Joshua Henkin, as well as from Andrea Barrett whom I first encountered at the

Bread Loaf Writers' Conference in 1984 and who has become a much-valued close colleague and friend. When previous students are mentioned—Bret Easton Ellis, Ted Mooney, David Shields—I smile and nod with that faintly avuncular proprietary interest of the previously involved. And other authors in this series—Frederick Busch, George Garrett, and Jon Manchip White, to name just three with whom I stay in touch—feel like comrades-in-arms on a long march indeed; we keep on keeping on.

This is one of the less celebrated pleasures and rewards of art. I don't of course know what it would feel like to be expert at appendix-extraction or real-estate contracts or stock-market trades—but I harbor the suspicion that repetition of those labors would soon or late wear thin. Practice makes, if not perfect, a practitioner accustomed to routine—but I have never yet felt boredom in the presence of a page. Anxiety, yes, frustration, yes, disappointment or satisfaction and even delight—but not boredom while I blacken what was blank before.

Nor can I envision retirement from the work of words. Ford Madox Ford called himself, after Hokusai (though he transferred the art from painting to prose), "an old man mad about writing." This seems exactly what to hope for from the literary life. The "chorale" of which I wrote means different voices, different registers; it means we make our music of what was once unsung.

*

The books I've produced should speak for themselves, and in any case I've written of them elsewhere; let me be brief. Since 1985 I've published two works of nonfiction; one more is about to appear. The first, a travel-text-cum-memoir, is called *Running in Place: Scenes from the South of France* (1987). A journey through both space and time, it reconstructed years spent in Provence—and in some ways signaled what has become an ongoing preoccupation in my work. Early on I stayed far from home base or, at the least, disguised it; lately I've been writing a good deal closer to home. Autobiography is, I think, a young and old author's game—but in what I hope to call my "middle" years I seem to have grown more inward-facing and, in *The Lost Suitcase,* self-reflexive.

This is a collection of essays with, at its center, a novella; the subtitle suggests an occupation and preoccupation both: *Reflections on the Literary Life* (2000). *The Countess of Stanlein Restored,* (2001), originally commissioned as an article for *Harper's Magazine,* is a short book that in some degree harkens back to *The Beaux Arts Trio: A Portrait.* My father-in-law, Bernard Greenhouse, owns the "Countess of Stanlein ex-Paganini Stradivarius Violoncello of 1707," and this account recounts, in detail, the meticulous restoration of that great instrument by the luthier René Morel. At eighty-four, Greenhouse still practices each morning; at ninety-one my father, Kurt Delbanco, goes daily to his studio to paint . . .

Further, I have published four books of "creative" as opposed to reportorial prose. *The Writers' Trade & Other Stories* (1990) is to my mind a companion-text to *About My Table & Other Stories* (1983). The earlier volume, as its title indicates, focused on the domestic life, the more recent the professional. Nine stories linked not so much by characters as vocation, it "bookends" what went before. After the Sherbrookes trilogy (1977–80) it felt as though the well went dry—or, at least, that book-length fictions (of which I'd published ten in a row) were no longer my métier.

So it would take a full fifteen years before I returned to the genre, with *In the Name of Mercy* (1995). An issue-driven novel, it follows on *News* (1970) as an attempt to engage a public issue with a public text; my topic here was euthanasia—in a state dominated at that time by the actions of Jack Kevorkian, the wild-eyed "Dr. Death." I tried to write it as a murder-mystery, and there's a good deal of mayhem entailed, but the real yield of the endeavor was that it introduced me to a new publisher and editor, Larry Kirshbaum and Jamie Raab of Warner Books. For both of them (as well as for my ongoing friendship with James Landis, who has long since left William Morrow) I remain grateful indeed.

The second of my novels published by Warner Books, *Old Scores* (1997), feels to its author like a reprise of *Small Rain* (1975). That text had as backstory the tale of Tristan and Iseult; the urtext in this instance is the history of Abelard and Heloise, updated and transposed to New England. "Catamount College" is a not-so-well-disguised reconstruction of Bennington, and in *Old Scores* I returned to the scene of the Sherbrookes trilogy—the mountains I stare at while writing these lines, the old white clapboard houses and meadows of Vermont. Most recently, the novel *What Remains*—to be published in November 2000—revisits the landscape of childhood, and London in the blitz. When my Uncle Gustav died in 1997, at ninety-three, I felt myself one of the remaining few articulate witnesses to that period and place. And whether this is true or not, I found myself hearing phrases at night—"Greedy blighter, silly billy"—that I'd not heard in fifty years from my exasperated elder brother, Tom . . .

Again I refer to this postscript's precursor, and 1985. Much of my new book derives from and expands upon that essay and those early memories. "I have written of this obliquely," I wrote, when writing of my mother's death. "Someday perhaps I will face it head on and at length. The roses on the Meissen and the Rosenthal, the roses on the library table, the horsehair mattress with the ineradicable blood-stains of my brother's birth, the martinis we shared, her love of the mountains, of reading, of chess— the sense I had from first awareness of her imperial adoration and ambition channeled through her sons, so that nothing but the best was good enough, and that only barely, from clothing to girlfriends to grades—the legacy is palpable. I scattered her ashes; that's all."

In *What Remains* I did "face it head on and at length," reconstructing the landscape in which I was born and the community of German Jewish refugees in Hampstead in the aftermath of war. As Ezra Pound put it in *The Pisan Cantos,* "What thou lovest well remains. The rest is dross . . ."

By way of keeping my hand in or sticking to the writer's last I've also served as editor these years. I've edited two volumes of Selected Hopwood Lectures and, with Laurence Goldstein, a book called *Writers and Their Craft*. As testimonial to the dear dead, I introduced and edited two novels by John Gardner and, with Alan Cheuse, the literary speculations of Bernard Malamud. Alan Cheuse became my colleague at Bennington in 1970; he first encouraged me to try my hand at nonfiction, and I remain in his debt.

One other relatively new component of the writing life— at least for me—has been the "business" of contests. Two years ago I served as Chair of the Fiction Panel of the National Book Awards; last year I was one of three judges for the PEN/Hemingway prize for first fiction, and this year for the PEN/Faulkner Award. This means that, roughly speaking, I've read—or at least held in my hand—some thousand books of contemporary American fiction in the past three years alone. It's a daunting prospect as well as retrospect; I've been grateful for the chance to celebrate the achievement of others and to assess the work of my contemporaries, as well as of elders and juniors—but enough's enough. My next project is a teaching text—a book more than tentatively titled *The Sincerest Form* and based on the strategies of imitation; it seems to me a useful way to study our great predecessors and to acquire via emulation the elements of style. I do hope to reach, as I begin to think about retirement, young writers I will never meet in a shared classroom space.

The word *refrain* is double-edged if not oxymoronic; as a descriptive term in ballad or song it means "repeat/reprise"; as an imperative it means "cease/withdraw." Though I called these lines a "postscript and addendum," they do seem a sort of refrain. To know that I've been teaching for longer than most of my students have lived is to contemplate redundancy, the deep paralysis of repetition, and to know that these last seven words ("contemplate redundancy, the deep paralysis of repetition") are both arcane and echoic is to start to stop . . .

Autobiography: Part III
(February 2017)

Fifteen years elapsed between the first and second of these efforts; the addendum was composed some seventeen years ago. Now this seems, for several reasons, the proper time and place to pick up the slack of the tale. I think of Clotho, Lachesis, Atropos— the three Fates who spin, draw out, and cut the thread of life. With luck, I won't soon again meet the last, but the first two ladies have long since grown familiar. Most of the folk I reported on in previous pages are dead: my parents, my in-laws, too many of my friends. Frederick Busch, George Garrett, Jon Manchip White—the three colleagues I referred to as companions in "Addendum"—all have "gone before." John Updike did so too. I refer here only to those authors named in previous essays, while still alive; were I to add other authors (Jo Carson, Ed Doctorow, Peter Matthiessen, James Salter, Arturo Vivante et al.), that "royal fellowship of death" would be twice as long . . .

Happily, by contrast, my wife and I have watched our daughters grow and marry and have daughters of their own. Life goes on. In the pages that follow I'll fill in these blanks, but where before I wished for more of the same, I must now report on change.

*

Let me begin with professional life; in June 2015, I retired from the University of Michigan with the daunting official title of the Robert Frost Distinguished University Professor of English Language and Literature and Professor Emeritus of English Language and Literature, College of Literature, Science, and the Arts. Given that I was first employed at Bennington in 1966, this made one short of fifty years in a profession I began by trying on for size and thought of as provisional. Once habituated to it, and happy in the practice, I told myself I'd retire when I'd been teaching since any of my undergraduates were born.

By 2015 I'd been doing so as long as many of their parents were alive, and it seemed time to stop. My beloved colleague Charles Baxter had left; the younger ones I'd hired—Michael Byers, Peter Ho Davies et al.—have succeeded at "the succession." Too, the fledgling MFA I came to Ann Arbor to build has grown into an imposing edifice. In response to a munificent gift—some sixty million dollars—the MFA was newly named (in honor of its donor) the Helen Zell Writer's Program. My dream—that no apprentice author would have to go into debt to study writing—has been realized, and the three-year program now flourishes without me.

By definition, nearly (unless one takes into account the lectures and appearances preserved for later viewing), a teacher teaches only those students who sit in a shared room. And as the years and rooms increased, I found myself hoping to reach those young or old adepts of literature and language whom I might never meet. It seemed right to put in writing the "accumulated wisdom" (these quotes are meant to suggest the tongue-in-cheek) of a career spent in class.

This resulted in two textbooks, *The Sincerest Form: Writing Fiction by Imitation* (McGraw-Hill, 2003) and *Literature: Craft and Voice,* a three-volume textbook which I co-edited with Alan Cheuse (McGraw-Hill, 2010) and which came out two years later as a single volume. With Alan I earlier edited *Talking Horse: Bernard Malamud on Life and Work* (Columbia University Press, 1996) and, with Laurence Goldstein, *Writers and Their Craft: Short Stories and Essays on the Narrative* (Wayne State University Press, 1991).

Add to that a series of collected Lectures and Prized Writings from the Hopwood Awards Program (four volumes in all, each published by the University of Michigan Press) and my first such venture, a posthumous compilation of fiction by John Gardner (Alfred A. Knopf, 1986) and I've been busy these past years with the prose of other authors. The first few of these transpired before my "Addendum" was published, and are referred to there. But I'm struck now, recapitulating, by how much time was spent on editorial work. It's honorable labor, and has kept me at the desk, yet sometimes I stare at the books on a shelf and wonder how and why I managed to accumulate so many of them, row on row. The mirror belies this, of course, but I still feel like that youngster who thought the world would change when a book by Delbanco appeared.

It hasn't—or not for the better. Nuclear disarmament remains conjectural; poverty and hate and violent conflicts remain; dictators and human traffickers and drug dealers thrive. Our national upheaval as of the last election is, I fear, something to fear. The climate (both actual and metaphoric) grows more heated, year by year. Twenty-fifteen was the hottest year on record, and though these old bones welcome warmth, I remember with real fondness the blizzards of my youth. For those of us—an increasing number—who have outlived our biblical span, the eighth decade is full of contradiction: each day we both add and subtract. One more entails one less.

Since the year 2000 I have published several novels: *What Remains* (2000), *The Vagabonds* (2004), *Spring and Fall* (2006), *The Count of Concord* (2008), a one-volume revised version of *Sherbrookes* (2011), and *The Years* (2015); I have two more on the desk as works-in-progress, one tentatively titled *The Work of Love* and another, perhaps fittingly, called *It Is Enough*. Over the years I convinced myself that each new project was a departure: I was shifting ground each time I sat to the desk. And it's to a degree true that *In the Name of Mercy* (a medical thriller) differs from *The Count of Concord* (a historical novel), and so on and so forth. But a writer's work is always more like his or her own other work than that of anyone else; we leave our fingerprints and rhetoric-tracks all over every page. So all these pieces deal with what I've come to recognize as recurrent themes: tradition and displacement, the interplay of generations and individual identity. All of them too, in one way or another, deal with the matter of love. Inexhaustible subjects, each, and book by book in this regard may perhaps be read as variations on a theme.

Mine is a minor career. This is neither falsely modest nor self-pitying as an assertion; it's the flat fact that most of the reading public (with the exception, perhaps, of those who write) read other authors instead. I used to mind this, used to want to change the terms of the equation while bellowing my own high-pitched *Me, me me me me!* Over the years and decades, however, such shrill urgency abates. There seem two ways to assess professional standing: (a) in comparative and (b) in absolute terms. By the comparative measure, perhaps, I've not done as well or as much as earlier hoped; this week's "genius" is overpraised, and it's hard not to feel some competitive impatience while hearing the applause. There are prizes I've not won and honors I have not accrued and languages into which I haven't been translated, and so on and so forth; it's easy to compile a set of slights . . .

Easy, but wrong. One writes for the joy of it, the benison of self-expression—and to do so uncensored for a long life is a great gift. In absolute terms, moreover, I've been fortunate to enter at all in the lists. It's a laziness of language that I call myself a writer when Shakespeare can be described by the same word. Think of great practitioners such as Balzac, Chekhov, or Melville, and I've nothing to complain of: to claim those men as predecessors is to be richly privileged, and the din and bustle of the marketplace subsides.

Nor is an author's career a competition in the sense of "winner take all," or "heavyweight champion of prose"—that delusory standard set by Hemingway, Mailer, and the rest; a writer doesn't win by defeating others or hoping they will lose. Even the phrase "an author's career" has a faintly timeworn feel to it, and the ring of anachrony; given the tweets and blogs and self-published memoirs that proliferate today, it has never been simpler to write. Anybody can anoint himself as author, appoint herself the at-least-momentary arbiter of standards and say, "Here's my book." On the other hand, it's never been more difficult to be a professional writer and make of the profession a life. The idea of a career has changed; a second book (unless the first was a commercial success) grows more difficult to publish than had been the first. Not to mention a seventh or tenth. What I was fortunate enough to do is something few can do today—expect that the next text, and the subsequent one, will be properly published and by strangers read.

"The death of the novel" has been so long predicted and so often disproved that the phrase comes to feel, a little, like Chicken Little's warning that the sky is falling. It hasn't happened yet, of course, and more books are being published now than was the case ever before. The graphic novel nowadays bears only a distant relation to the work of Joseph Fielding; what *Pride and Prejudice* and *Fifty Shades of Grey* have in common is only the category to which they by genre belong. More accurate to say that, Phoenix-like, the form is constantly reborn. So it's foolish as well as fruitless to lament the passing of a mode to which one aspired when young, and many of my students—Jesmyn Ward, who won the National Book Award for her second novel, Chigozie Obioma, who was short-listed for the Booker Prize for his first—have good reason to believe that their careers will prosper.

But I can't shake the sense that the profession I entered is not the one that at present exists; the industry itself has altered almost beyond recognition. And I can't say, in simple truth, that I would have persevered in this long-cherished privacy had I known, fifty years ago, what I know today. More likely I would have done what so many of the young now do—turned to television writing in New York or screenplays in Los Angeles—and worked in collaboration with others. That the epicenter of "the writer's trade" has shifted in my lifetime seems inarguable; there's energy abounding in those related genres, and the novel and the novelist are, if not irrelevant, bit players in the show. To write a best-seller nowadays is to have thousands of readers; to market a successful film requires millions who stand in line to pay. To maintain one's calling as an artist in unpublished isolation is quixotic if not obsessional, and only a fortunate few can stay, as it were, in the game.

My last two books of nonfiction, indeed, dealt with these topics as subjects. The first, *Lastingness: The Art of Old Age* (2011) considered men and women who at least maintained and in some cases advanced their art past the age of seventy. For obvious reasons, that's a subject of incremental interest to me—but I followed it with a study of *The Art of Youth: Crane, Carrington, Gershwin, and the Nature of First Acts* (2013). It seems in retrospect peculiar that I should have reversed, if only in chronological terms, the sequence of those inquiries and not followed the progression these two topics represent. Near the end of *The Art of Youth,* however, I offer these lines on the long-distant past:

> I married a girl from America whose allegiance is to Cape Cod. I open littlenecks and oysters now with a less practiced wrist; I've not seen or eaten—much less delivered—a hand-harpooned swordfish in years. I no longer teach at Bennington or call New England home. Much changes and has changed. But the labor of writing a sentence, rewriting it, *rewriting* it is still a labor I love.

*

Time now to write of generations, tradition, and displacement. That all of us are born to die is scarcely news, yet it still comes as a shock. The death of my friend Alan Cheuse is very hard to accept. He was vividly alive. No one I ever knew was more imbued with hopeful energy, a resolute stick-to-itiveness and the desire to savor the world. So many projects on his desk, so much to be achieved. His first question to me, always, was "What are you writing?" And then, "What have you read?"

I knew Alan for forty-five years; we met when he was starting out as both a writer and teacher. We were colleagues at Bennington College, in the Bennington Writing Workshops, and at the University of Michigan—where he taught from 1984 to 1986. He succeeded George Garrett and preceded me as Acting Director of the then-fledgling MFA Program in Writing. I don't think a week went by in the past several decades without my hearing Alan's voice on the phone or, lately, in an email and text-message exchange; he was animated always, always engaged and involved.

Which makes it all the harder to believe him gone. The day before he tried to drive—with what turned out to be fatal exhaustion—from Squaw Valley down to Santa Cruz, he told me he would do so; the day after the accident I spoke to him in the Santa Clara Hospital, and he was (though a touch groggy from drugs) still very much himself. We joked about how lucky he was that all he suffered were three cracked ribs and a neck-brace he'd be wearing while the sixth vertebra healed; we agreed that things could have been worse. And then they got much worse. The coma into which he fell and from which he failed to wake put an end to his earthly existence, though not to his survival in my heart and on the page.

As suggested at this segment's start, he joins a lengthy list. Jon Manchip White, of whom I also wrote in the two previous installments, died at the age of eighty-nine on 31 July 2013—two years to the day before the death of Alan Cheuse. Our lengthy correspondence was collected and reprinted in *Dear Wizard: The Letters of Nicholas Delbanco and Jon Manchip White* (University of Michigan Press, 2014); it details a friendship full of epistolary high-jinx and a shared commitment to our shared profession. When I think of those who joined me at the inception of the Bennington Writing Workshops in the summer of 1977—Stephen Becker, John Cheever, John Gardner, Bernard Malamud, not to mention those who spoke in the ensuing years—Hortense Calisher, Ralph Ellison, Thomas Flanagan, Grace Paley, Mark Strand, Charlie Williams and too many others to name—I am the sole survivor. It chastens and dispirits me to feel this way, but more of my colleagues are dead than alive, and much of my attitude is elegiac. It shocks me still—who was, it seemed, always the youngest—to be, routinely now, the oldest in the room. This is the way of the world, of course, for all of us who live long lives; the nonagenarian and centenarian—increasing as a cadre these years—have multitudes to mourn.

So it's doubly and trebly a gift to watch those who enter the world. I thought long and hard about marriage, thought with a degree of attentive concern about the prospect of fatherhood, but becoming and being a grandfather was never "on my screen." It took me by surprise. And—no surprise—it's the unmediated pleasure everyone describes; our five granddaughters have been, daily and yearly, a blessing. Anna Delbanco Shalom is nine years old as of this writing, and living with her seven-year-old sister Rosalie Delbanco Shalom in South Orange, New Jersey; their mother Andrea is an executive editor at *TIME for Kids* magazine in New York. Penelope Aurora Stoller is also nine, her sister Frederica Bernadette Stoller is three; the newest arrival, Lydia Franklin Stoller, is barely three months old. Their mother Francesca lives in Los Angeles. Andrea's husband, Alexander Shalom, is a lawyer for the ACLU in New Jersey; Francesca's husband, Nicholas Stoller, is a movie writer/director/producer, and the two of them are now engaged in television as well.

When I first wrote about Andrea, she was the age of her younger daughter and a "passionate, spark-sending imp"; as the mother of two daughters she's the very image of competent authority, and I cannot help marveling at her prowess at work and at home. Francesca, for whom I predicted a career in language or the theater, has fulfilled those predictions, and then some; her novel *Ask Me Anything* (W. W. Norton, 2004) and her life on or near the red carpet is all a fond father could dream of. When we gather as a family, what the granddaughters call "the cousins' club" is a source of unending delight.

Its *primum mobile* is, of course, my wife. We've become a cottage industry. Elena, too, has published a successful novel—*The Silver Swan* (Other Press, 2015), and I'm button-busting proud of her achievement; when she retired from her position in the Ford School of Public Policy at the University of Michigan, she simply sat down and wrote, in a great burst of focused energy, a book about the world of classical musicians—a world she'd witnessed since birth. So that sense of diminution I wrote of in my own career has been happily supplanted by the expansion of hers; as a tribe, we thrive. To move from the first-person pronoun to the plural or collective—to shift from "I" to "we"—is a welcome by-product of older age: the slackening ego expands. Perhaps it's a form of osmosis: the semipermeable membrane of the self grows newly nourished by surroundings, and the *me me me* becomes *us*.

Geography figured largely in my previous installments; it does so, still. As of this writing, the compass tilts eastward; we purchased a small apartment in New York City, overlooking the Hudson River and up by Columbia's campus—where I was a graduate student and where, from time to time, I teach a Master Class. More importantly, perhaps, we have renovated the house in Wellfleet, Massachusetts, where Elena's parents lived and died, and which we now call home. Old ghosts have been spelled and new wiring put in; the walls are newly insulated and the bathrooms free of mold. The marsh beneath, the bay beyond, the brilliant morning light and slowly lengthening evening shade—all these are Gilead's balm.

*

The village of Wellfleet on Cape Cod spans a land-spit three miles wide. It sits between Cape Cod Bay and the Atlantic Ocean; freshwater ponds lie between. The vegetation is salt-laved: scrub oak and pine, cranberry, bayberry, poison ivy. The hills are low, the dunes high. Much of the area has been protected by the Cape Cod National Sea Shore, but all remains at risk: the roads are clogged with traffic, the aquifer diminishes, and the cliffs erode. In this fragile ecosystem, the issue of garbage disposal is of major consequence, and what used to be the "town dump" is now an elaborate facility for which one pays an annual fee, and to which I make a pilgrimage each week.

It's no casual procedure. Most of us have long accepted the concept of recycling and that it makes sense to reduce the amount of waste we as consumers produce. Increasingly, we divide what can be salvaged from what we consign to a landfill; we separate glass from newspaper and plastic and used food. But the Wellfleet Transfer Center and Recycling Station carries this practice to extremes, and to pass through its portals—a gate unlocked at posted hours and a long drive up a hill with a guardhouse at its summit, where one's permit is inspected by a quasi-military sentry—is to relinquish choice. A portable radio blares; the compacting processors hum. There are great green bins with labels— Newspaper and Cardboard, Plastic and Tin—that are compacted on site. There are tables for empty bottles and jam jars and clear and colored glass containers, as well as buckets where you leave the caps and corks. There's a table for used light-bulbs and one for worn-out batteries; there are men who supervise this process of distribution and tell you what you've done wrong.

Wearing yellow armbands and green vests, they monitor particular items for specialized disposal, pointing to the further reaches of the site. There are places where oyster shells get dropped, spaces for yard waste and Styrofoam and tree stumps, locales for metal and window screens and window glass and used electronic devices. A TV set or broken microwave oven will cost ten dollars to dispose of at a designated shed; there's a "Swap Shop"—open every other afternoon, from 2 to 5—where you can deposit books or old CDs or furniture that someone else might welcome, and forage for leavings you then carry home. These items must pass the hard muster of the sentinel within.

Finally, there is a reeking pair of thirty-foot-long sunken metal containers where you throw your trash. This must be bagged in special purple plastic sacks (small, medium-sized, or large available for purchase in the Wellfleet Market), and when the receptacles are filled to capacity, they get forklifted onto sixteen-wheelers and trundled off the cape. Grizzled locals in their pick-up trucks will sometimes violate protocol and dare to throw a cardboard box or mattress over the protective fence and down into the bins. But part-time residents—this one, at any rate— tend to follow orders. Indeed, I take a kind of pride when watchmen nod approval at how well I've separated the plastic bottles for recycling from those that can be returned for deposit, how thoroughly I've rinsed a jar of marmalade or a tin can of beans.

Katharine Boo, in her 2012 Pulitzer prize–winning account *Beyond the Beautiful Forevers,* details, as her subtitle suggests, "Life, death and hope in a Mumbai undercity." There she describes the camaraderie and competition of a group of dump-dwellers who forage for survival. In our prosperous nation, the stakes are less high—but there's still a cadre of those who pick over what others discard and, as the old song puts it, "get some cash for your trash." These "regulars" sip cans of soda and complain about the weather and traffic and rehearse the Wellfleet news. I sidle up and grin at them, making what I think of as informed remarks about the town council or the power company's clear-cutting or the run of striped bass and bluefish—remarks which are, invariably, greeted by affable absolute silence. They stare and turn away.

I leave. Driving back down the hill from the landfill, windows shut against the stench of it, I congratulate myself on having completed my task and, in so doing, helped to organize the planet. "The order of ordure"—I try out a phrase—"the composition of compost, the transfer of trash, way of waste." There's something deeply gratifying about such distribution: every item has its place and all can be redeemed.

This is absurd, of course: we make small difference here. Rumor has it that the sixteen-wheelers hauling garbage lump everything together after our dutiful sorting. And day by week by month the waste accumulates. But as the air clears and I open the car windows, I'm seized by the conviction that what I've done is similar to what I also do each day: distribute words on a page. Writers attempt to make sense—phrase by sentence by paragraph by chapter—of the arrangement of language; we try to fashion order out of jumbled inexactness. An adjective here, a pair of adverbs there, a dangling participle or inexact parallel clause—all these must be examined, then pruned. In the interests of clarity, each overlong sentence can be compacted and by editing reduced.

When I enter that guarded compound—the Wellfleet Transfer Station and Recycling Center—I'm subject to inspection as well as introspection; when I leave, I leave with a sentence both processed and complete. And can start piling trash for the next.

*

Last February I died. Briefly, and two or three times. Then I returned to life and, soon enough, this desk. Because I write these sentences, it's clear my demise was impermanent, transient, and that I've survived. "Flatlining" is a medical condition, not all that infrequent after a heart-bypass operation and an aortic-valve replacement, both of which I had. This fact—extraordinary to me yet routine to the members of the ICU Code Blue team— remains the salient statement of the year. So I'm happy beyond simple saying to report I'm on the mend. But it's been a long trajectory and should be briefly described. What follows is both coda and reprise:

On 25 February 2016, I checked into the Frankel Cardiovascular Center at the University of Michigan Hospital for a planned operation on my heart. Doctors G. Michael Deeb and Francis Pagani were the tag team of eminent surgeons; in this age of specialization, the latter would deal with a double coronary bypass, the former with a valve replacement. They would "harvest" a vein from my right leg for the arterial tissue and, where the aorta met the upper chamber of the heart, deploy a bovine valve. All this had been explained to me at painstaking length in the weeks before; my arteries had been occluded since at least 2003, when I had the first two stents inserted in an angioplasty, and the mild aortic stenosis was growing critical. In surgeon-speak, the doctor had explained to me that there was good news and bad. The good news was that, nowadays, my problems could be remedied; the bad is that, without intervention, I'd likely have a lethal heart attack.

So surgery wasn't elective; I knew it had to be done. For a dozen years or so I'd lived with the band of pain in my chest, a debilitating anxiety that never quite amounted to a medical imperative; it was, or so I told myself, an inescapable aspect of increasing age. Others noticed. I grew slower, paler, plumper—but the first three symptoms of heart trouble are "Denial, denial, denial." And so I soldiered on, walking through what had become habitual discomfort, feeling cold in my fingers and toes, taking naps. Yet at December's end I reached the point where denial no longer made sense. The good news—to continue with that surgical trope—is that my heart remained undamaged and this was no emergency; the bad news was I therefore had to wait.

Which, for two months, my wife and I did. Each time I lifted weight or climbed a hill or set of stairs, I sensed the heart's exertion; each flight we took I feared. It's a strange state—uneasiness compounded by anxiety, yet a sense of resignation and the desire not to raise a false alarm. I imagine much of humanity lives with this accommodation: a pain in the wrist or shoulder or head if not heart. In Hamlet's terms, I told myself, these were "the thousand natural shocks that flesh is heir to"; in Delbanco's terms, however, it felt like a death sentence not quite yet pronounced. And so I waited, less and less patiently, for the appointed date.

The night before, snow fell. It was the sort of storm that, earlier, I'd discount and shovel or brush my way through. But the six inches of new snow seemed newly perilous, and we wondered if the hospital would continue to function in this mini-blizzard, or if we could reach it at, as scheduled, 6:00 a.m. I packed a bag full of what turned out to be supernumerary items: a book, a pair of pajamas, the *New York Times,* a toothbrush—none of which would be needed or serviceable for the next few days. Then, in the predawn dark, we drove to the University of Michigan's Frankel Cardiovascular Center and were ushered in. There were smiling folk at the Service Desk, pots of coffee brewing; there was classical music playing, original art on the walls. This was the last time for a month I would be permitted to drive, and I remember relinquishing the car keys with a sense of near-fatality: when if ever might I take the steering wheel and driver's seat again?

I signed forms. I produced proof of identity and power of attorney sheets and renounced the right to sue. Elena and I embraced; then I went inside to be "prepped." Over the next few hours, I put myself in the hands of nameless friendly func-tionaries—nameless in that, though I promised myself not to, I kept forgetting their names. There were male and female nurses, anesthesiologists, folks who kept asking me for my own name and date of birth and medical history and understanding of the procedure to come; I put my clothes in plastic bags—no wed-ding ring or watch or wallet, please!—and my body hair was shaved and I was hooked up to various IV drips and sedated and wheeled away on a gurney.

The operation went well. It was, I think, much harder on my wife than on her husband— because she remained conscious and anxious for the eight-hour procedure, whereas I was wholly anes-thetized and only came around again once they'd removed my breathing tube and reattached my heart.

That first night is largely a blur; I woke or was awakened every few hours by ICU personnel while Elena slept fitfully beside me in a Barcalounger. My principal fear had been that of stroke—a diminished awareness—and I was glad to do my multiplication tables and silently recite brief passages of poetry and remember the names of the thirty-two authors I'd interviewed for the text-book *Craft & Voice*. There were IVs and a Foley Catheter and a pressurized wrapping on my leg and various bruises and ban-dages, but by and large I felt fine.

On Friday morning the surgeon on his rounds confirmed this and promised to send me upstairs for the next stage of recovery, leaving the ICU. A social worker arrived to talk about making arrangements for a Visiting Nurse once I was sent home; she was affable, instructive, and Elena and I were smiling, chatting, glad to make the plans.

*

Then I flopped back and collapsed. I can remember, dimly, feeling like a fish on planks, convulsive although in no obvious pain. Of a sudden, the room filled. Elena had cried out; so, no doubt, had the mechanical monitors. A gaggle of blue-coated personnel flew in. There were many of them; one barked orders, others followed; faces loomed. I knew I was in trouble and can remember asking, more than once, "Am I going to die?" I can remember, also, asking the people in attendance please to take care of my wife. Those two phrases—the question "Am I going to die?" and the statement "Tell Elena not to worry"—are all I recall repeating amid the fuss and noise. I was told later that I remained calm, but *calm* seems only an approximate description of the state I entered: a distance, a remoteness, a valedictory desire to survive and thereafter return.

There ensued a quasi-military drill: a Nurse Practitioner called Courtney who supervised the procedure, a series of men and women who obeyed her, others who looked on. For obvious reasons—my sternum had been sliced open, then provisionally wired shut again—they couldn't use the standard techniques of resuscitation: paddles or pressure applied to the chest. Instead, they used electrical stimuli and drugs. I recollect what I can only call pinpricks of light—a series of shocks in my stomach that somehow I could *see* as well as feel. I saw that long tunnel they write of, and bright whiteness at the end of it; I watched a blur of blue-clad bodies until I closed my eyes.

They wheeled me to another section of the hospital where—in and out of focus—I underwent an additional procedure. Technicians affixed a temporary pacemaker to the right side of my neck; this was supposed to remedy my irregular heartbeat, if needed; a young Chinese woman held a blue cloth above my eyes so I would not be blinded by the arc-lights beating down. (Was this, I wonder, an explanation for that white blaze at tunnel's end? Is the vision of life after death merely a reaction to bright ceiling lights?) Repeatedly, she apologized for both her clumsiness and her poor English; repeatedly I told her that she was doing fine. That little metal box—screwed in and taped to my neck—felt like a vampire bat.

The rest is quickly told. Both body and mind shut down, a bit, when confined to a hospital bed and room; the next days remain a dull blur. Small victories like learning to roll one's hips to the edge of the bed, to brush one's teeth, to walk the hall— first pushing a wheelchair, then a walker, then unaided—are a litany of recovery-steps familiar to anyone who has confronted them. There's the daily round of visitors and nurses on succeeding shifts and pills and naps to take and meals to order and then eat and television shows to watch; these are absorbing to engage in perhaps, but less so to describe. The week wore on. When they removed my pacemaker and had me stand to weigh myself and sent me to PT to climb a flight of stairs, I knew my time of cosseted interiority was drawing to a close.

Throughout I'd had unsettling visions of those less fortunate than I—the hundreds of thousands of wounded or ill around the world or in this country with no access to medical facilities, or lying on stone floors or mud or sand or rubble awaiting momentary attention from overworked doctors and nurses—unable to pay for or get sustained help. I was lucky; I knew it; I know it; my gratitude is tinged with guilt at having been so privileged. And to belong now, once again, to the quick not dead.

*

One final scene. At the height of the fuss and ruckus of resuscitation, Elena was urged into the corridor; there were too many personnel in the room, and her obviously distraught presence might complicate their drill. She stood in the ICU hall. The large doors at the end of it slid open noiselessly; a woman walked towards her, pushing a small harp and stool on a table with wheels. "Would you like some music?" she inquired.

My wife said, "Not now, no. Any instrument, please, but the harp!"

Oblivious, the volunteer unpacked her equipment and, sitting, commenced to play. My wife loves music and knows a great deal about it but did not know how to say "Stop!" While the medical emergency within the room was attended to and dealt with, she endured an impromptu concert performed by a tone-deaf, smiling, nodding musician who plucked at the harp-strings by way of comfort.

Then, after a suitable interval, the lady packed up and moved on.

Acknowledgments

"The Countess of Stanlein Restored" appeared in *Harper's Magazine*, January 2001.

"A Visit to the Gallery" appeared in *Raritan: A Quarterly Review* 27, no. 3.

"My Old Young Books" is the postscript to the Dalkey Archive Edition of *Sherbrookes*, 2011; it was also published, in somewhat different form, in *The Writer's Chronicle*, February 2011.

"Towards an Autobiography" has three component parts: the first appeared in the Gale Research Company's *Contemporary Authors Autobiography Series*, Volume 2, the second in Volume 189. Collectively, the series is known as *A Bio-Bibliographical Guide to Current Writers in Fiction, General Nonfiction, Poetry, Journalism, Drama, Motion Pictures, Television, and Other Fields.*

21ST CENTURY ESSAYS

David Lazar and Patrick Madden, Series Editors

A new series from The Ohio State University Press, 21st Century Essays is a vehicle to discover, publish, and promote some of the most daring, ingenious, and artistic new nonfiction. This is the first and only major series that announces its focus on the essay—a genre whose plasticity, timelessness, popularity, and centrality to nonfiction writing make it especially important in the field of nonfiction literature. In addition to publishing the most interesting and innovative books of essays by American writers, the series will publish extraordinary international essayists and reprint works by neglected or forgotten essayists, voices that deserve to be heard, revived, and reprised. The series is a major addition to the possibilities of contemporary literary nonfiction, focusing on that central, frequently chimerical, and invariably supple form: The Essay.

Curiouser and Curiouser
NICHOLAS DELBANCO

Don't Come Back
LINA MARÍA FERREIRA CABEZA-VANEGAS

A Mother's Tale
PHILLIP LOPATE